About the Author

Born in Germany, Edgar Rothermich studied music and soun[d] prestigious Tonmeister program at the Berlin Institute of Tech[nology] University of Arts (UdK) in Berlin where he graduated in 1989 with a Master's Degree. He worked as a composer and music producer in Berlin, and moved to Los Angeles in 1991 where he continued his work on numerous projects in the music and film industry ("The Celestine Prophecy", "Outer Limits", "Babylon 5", "What the Bleep Do We Know", "Fuel", "Big Money Rustlas").

For over 20 years, Edgar has had a successful musical partnership with electronic music pioneer and founding Tangerine Dream member Christopher Franke. In addition to his collaboration with Christopher, Edgar has been working with other artists, as well as on his own projects.

In 2010 he started to release his solo records in the "Why Not ..." series with different styles and genres. The current releases are "Why Not Solo Piano", "Why Not Electronica", "Why Not Electronica Again", and "Why Not 90s Electronica". This previously unreleased album was produced in 1991/1992 by Christopher Franke. All albums are available on Amazon and iTunes, including the 2012 release, the re-recording of the Blade Runner Soundtrack.

In addition to composing music, Edgar Rothermich is writing technical manuals with a unique style, focusing on rich graphics and diagrams to explain concepts and functionality of software applications under his popular GEM series (Graphically Enhanced Manuals). His best-selling titles are available as printed books on Amazon, as Multi-Touch eBooks on the iBooks Store, and as pdf downloads from his website.

Since 2017, Edgar Rothermich is Adjunct Professor at the Fullerton College Fine Arts Department, teaching Electronic Music, Synthesis, Audio Production, Pro Tools, and Logic Pro.

www.DingDingMusic.com   GEM@DingDingMusic.com

● Special Thanks

Special thanks to my beautiful wife, Li, for her love, support, and understanding during those long hours of working on the books. And not to forget my son, Winston. Waiting for him during soccer practice or Chinese class always gives me extra time to work on a few chapters.

The manual is based on Logic Pro X v10.4.2
Manual: Print Version 2018-0928
ISBN-13: 978-1722841195
ISBN-10:1722841192

⬤ About the GEM (Graphically Enhanced Manuals)

UNDERSTAND, not just LEARN

What are Graphically Enhanced Manuals? They're a new type of manual with a visual approach that helps you UNDERSTAND a program, not just LEARN it. No need to read through 500 pages of dry text explanations. Rich graphics and diagrams help you to get that "aha" effect and make it easy to comprehend difficult concepts. The Graphically Enhanced Manuals help you master a program much faster with a much deeper understanding of concepts, features, and workflows in a very intuitive way that is easy to understand.

All titles are available in three different formats:

.... pdf downloads from my website www.DingDingMusic.com/Manuals

.... multi-touch iBooks on Apple's iBooks Store

.... printed books on Amazon.com

(some manuals are also available in Deutsch, Español, 简体中文)

For a list of all the available titles and bundles: www.DingDingMusic.com/Manuals

To be notified about new releases and updates, subscribe to subscribe@DingDingMusic.com

⬤ About the Formatting

I use a specific color code in my books:

Green colored text indicates keyboard shortcuts. I use the following abbreviations: **sh** (shift key), **ctr** (control key), **opt** (option key), **cmd** (command key). A plus (+) between the keys means that you have to press all those keys at the same time.

sh+opt+K means: Hold the shift and the option key while pressing the K key.

Blue colored text indicates an action with the mouse (click, double-click, drag, etc.) plus any modifier keys that need to be pressed down during that action. For example, *opt+drag*

Brown colored text indicates Menu Commands with a greater sign (➤) indicating submenus.

Edit ➤ Source Media ➤ All means "Click on the Edit Menu, scroll down to Source Media, and select the submenu All.

Dimmed Blue text indicates an important term

Condensed text indicates a command or a label.

Blue arrows indicate what happens if you click on an item or popup menu

Table of Contents

About This Book

Logic Pro X v10.4.2 has quite an impressive list of changes despite that this is "just" a point-release.

Official Release Notes

For a comprehensive list of all the new stuff, you can access the official Release Notes directly from inside Logic by selecting the Main Menu ***Help ➤ Release Notes***, which opens your web browser, displaying the list on Apple's website. https://support.apple.com/en-us/HT203718

Release Notes v10.4.2

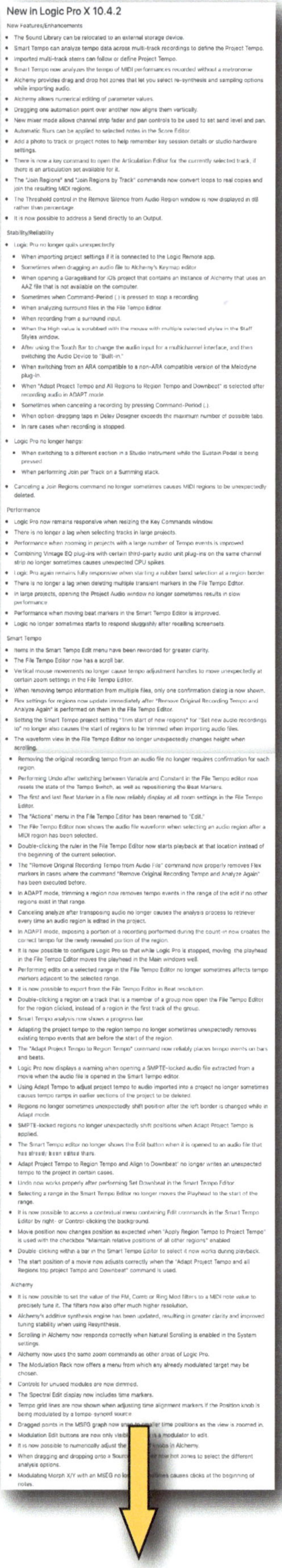
New in Logic Pro X 10.4.2

New Features/Enhancements

- The Sound Library can be relocated to an external storage device.
- Smart Tempo can analyze tempo data across multi-track recordings to define the Project Tempo.
- Imported multi-track stems can follow or define Project Tempo.
- Smart Tempo now analyzes the tempo of MIDI performances recorded without a metronome
- Alchemy provides drag and drop hot zones that let you select re-synthesis and sampling options while importing audio.
- Alchemy allows numerical editing of parameter values.
- Dragging one automation point over another now aligns them vertically.
- New mixer mode allows channel strip fader and pan controls to be used to set send level and pan.
- Automatic Slurs can be applied to selected notes in the Score Editor.
- Add a photo to track or project notes to help remember key session details or studio hardware settings.
- There is now a key command to open the Articulation Editor for the currently selected track, if there is an articulation set available for it.
- The "Join Regions" and "Join Regions by Track" commands now convert loops to real copies and join the resulting MIDI regions.
- The Threshold control in the Remove Silence from Audio Region window is now displayed in dB rather than percentage
- It is now possible to address a Send directly to an Output.

Stability/Reliability

- Logic Pro no longer quits unexpectedly
  - When importing project settings if it is connected to the Logic Remote app.
  - Sometimes when dragging an audio file to Alchemy's Keymap editor
  - When opening a GarageBand for iOS project that contains an instance of Alchemy that uses an AAZ file that is not available on the computer.
  - Sometimes when Command-Period (.) is pressed to stop a recording
  - When analyzing surround files in the File Tempo Editor.
  - When recording from a surround input.
  - When the High value is scrubbed with the mouse with multiple selected styles in the Staff Styles window.
  - After using the Touch Bar to change the audio input for a multichannel interface, and then switching the Audio Device to "Built-in."
  - When switching from an ARA compatible to a non-ARA compatible version of the Melodyne plug-in.
  - When "Adapt Project Tempo and All Regions to Region Tempo and Downbeat" is selected after recording audio in ADAPT mode.
  - Sometimes when canceling a recording by pressing Command-Period (.).
  - When option-dragging taps in Delay Designer exceeds the maximum number of possible tabs.
  - In rare cases when recording is stopped.
- Logic Pro no longer hangs:
  - When switching to a different section in a Studio Instrument while the Sustain Pedal is being pressed
  - When performing Join per Track on a Summing stack.
- Canceling a Join Regions command no longer sometimes causes MIDI regions to be unexpectedly deleted.

Performance

- Logic Pro now remains responsive when resizing the Key Commands window.
- There is no longer a lag when selecting tracks in large projects.
- Performance when zooming in projects with a large number of Tempo events is improved
- Combining Vintage EQ plug-ins with certain third-party audio unit plug-ins on the same channel strip no longer sometimes causes unexpected CPU spikes.
- Logic Pro again remains fully responsive when starting a rubber band selection at a region border.
- There is no longer a lag when deleting multiple transient markers in the File Tempo Editor.
- In large projects, opening the Project Audio window no longer sometimes results in slow performance
- Performance when moving beat markers in the Smart Tempo Editor is improved.
- Logic no longer sometimes starts to respond sluggishly after recalling screensets.

Smart Tempo

- Items in the Smart Tempo Edit menu have been reworded for greater clarity.
- The File Tempo Editor now has a scroll bar.
- Vertical mouse movements no longer cause tempo adjustment handles to move unexpectedly at certain zoom settings in the File Tempo Editor.
- When removing tempo information from multiple files, only one confirmation dialog is now shown.
- Flex settings for regions now update immediately after "Remove Original Recording Tempo and Analyze Again" is performed on them in the File Tempo Editor.
- Setting the Smart Tempo project setting "Trim start of new regions" for "Set new audio recordings to" no longer also causes the start of regions to be trimmed when importing audio files.
- The waveform view in the File Tempo Editor no longer unexpectedly changes height when scrolling.
- Removing the original recording tempo from an audio file no longer requires confirmation for each region.
- Performing Undo after switching between Variable and Constant in the File Tempo editor now resets the state of the Tempo Switch, as well as repositioning the Beat Markers.
- The first and last Beat Marker in a file now reliably display at all zoom settings in the File Tempo Editor.
- The "Actions" menu in the File Tempo Editor has been renamed to "Edit."
- The File Tempo Editor now shows the audio file waveform when selecting an audio region after a MIDI region has been selected.
- Double-clicking the ruler in the File Tempo Editor now starts playback at that location instead of the beginning of the current selection.
- The "Remove Original Recording Tempo from Audio File" command now properly removes Flex markers in cases where the command "Remove Original Recording Tempo and Analyze Again" has been executed before.
- In ADAPT mode, trimming a region now removes tempo events in the range of the edit if no other regions exist in that range.
- Canceling analyze after transposing audio no longer causes the analysis process to retriever every time an audio region is edited in the project.
- In ADAPT mode, exposing a portion of a recording performed during the count-in now creates the correct tempo for the newly revealed portion of the region.
- It is now possible to configure Logic Pro so that while Logic Pro is stopped, moving the playhead in the File Tempo Editor moves the playhead in the Main windows well.
- Performing edits on a selected range in the File Tempo Editor no longer sometimes affects tempo markers adjacent to the selected range.
- It is now possible to export from the File Tempo Editor in Beat resolution.
- Double-clicking a region on a track that is a member of a group now open the File Tempo Editor for the region clicked, instead of a region in the first track of the group.
- Smart Tempo analysis now shows a progress bar
- Adapting the project tempo to the region tempo no longer sometimes unexpectedly removes existing tempo events that are before the start of the region.
- The "Adapt Project Tempo to Region Tempo" command now reliably places tempo events on bars and beats.
- Logic Pro now displays a warning when opening a SMPTE-locked audio file extracted from a movie when the audio file is opened in the Smart Tempo editor.
- Using Adapt Tempo to adjust project tempo to audio imported into a project no longer sometimes causes tempo ramps in earlier sections of the project to be deleted.
- Regions no longer sometimes unexpectedly shift position after the left border is changed while in Adapt mode.
- SMPTE-locked regions no longer unexpectedly shift positions when Adapt Project Tempo is applied.
- The Smart Tempo editor no longer shows the Edit button when it is opened to an audio file that has already been edited there.
- Adapt Project Tempo to Region Tempo and Align to Downbeat' no longer writes an unexpected tempo to the project in certain cases.
- Undo now works properly after performing Set Downbeat in the Smart Tempo Editor
- Selecting a range in the Smart Tempo Editor no longer moves the Playhead to the start of the range.
- It is now possible to access a contextual menu containing Edit commands in the Smart Tempo Editor by right- or Control-clicking the background.
- Movie position now changes position as expected when "Apply Region Tempo to Project Tempo" is used with the checkbox "Maintain relative positions of all other regions" enabled
- Double-clicking within a bar in the Smart Tempo Editor to select it now works during playback.
- The start position of a movie now adjusts correctly when the "Adapt Project Tempo and all Regions top project Tempo and Downbeat" command is used.

Alchemy

- It is now possible to set the value of the FM, Comb or Ring Mod filters to a MIDI note value to precisely tune it. The filters now also offer much higher resolution.
- Alchemy's additive synthesis engine has been updated, resulting in greater clarity and improved tuning stability when using Resynthesis.
- Scrolling in Alchemy now responds correctly when Natural Scrolling is enabled in the System settings.
- Alchemy now uses the same zoom commands as other areas of Logic Pro.
- The Modulation Rack now offers a menu from which any already modulated target may be chosen.
- Controls for unused modules are now dimmed.
- The Spectral Edit display now includes time markers.
- Tempo grid lines are now shown when adjusting time alignment markers if the Position knob is being modulated by a tempo-synced source
- Dragged points in the MSEG graph now [illegible] time positions as the view is zoomed in.
- Modulation Edit buttons are now only visib[illegible] is a modulator to edit.
- It is now possible to numerically adjust the [illegible] knobs in Alchemy.
- When dragging and dropping onto a Sourc[illegible] now hot zones to select the different analysis options.
- Modulating Morph X/Y with an MSEG no lo[illegible] causes clicks at the beginning of notes.

Why this Book?

So why did I write this book when all the new features and improvements are listed in the official Release Notes?

Graphically Enhanced

The official Release Notes only provide a short one-line, text-only description of the new features and changes. In this book, I provide an in-depth explanation with lots of graphics, screenshots, diagrams, and sometimes additional detailed information on the topic to better understand the changes. You will immediately have a "clear picture" of the changes and additions and can start using them right away.

Hidden Features

The official Release Notes often forget to list a few features, so whatever additional changes I stumbled over, found online, or what other users discovered on the various Logic forums, I will also include here.

My other Logic Books

If you are new to my style of writing Graphically Enhanced Manuals and enjoy this book, don't forget to check out my other Logic books and my Graphically Enhanced Logic blog on my website http://LogicProGEM.com.

If you've never read any of my other books and you aren't familiar with my Graphically Enhanced Manuals (GEM) series, let me explain my approach. As I mentioned at the beginning, my motto is:

"UNDERSTAND, not just LEARN"

Other manuals (original User Guides or third party books) often provide just a quick way to: "press here and then click there, then that will happen ... now click over there, and something else will happen". This will go on for the next couple hundred pages, and all you'll do is memorize lots of steps without understanding the reason for doing them in the first place. Even more problematic is that you are stuck when you try to perform a procedure and the promised outcome doesn't happen. You will have no understanding why it didn't happen and, most importantly, what to do to make it happen.

Don't get me wrong, I'll also explain all the necessary procedures, but beyond that, the understanding of the underlying concept so you'll know the reason why you have to click here or there. Teaching you "why" develops a much deeper understanding of the application that later enables you, based on your knowledge, to react to "unexpected" situations. In the end, you will master the application.

And how do I provide that understanding? The key element is the visual approach, presenting easy to understand diagrams that describe an underlying concept better than five pages of text-only descriptions.

I mark important terms in this manual with a gray font. Try to memorize those terms or descriptions because that is the language you are using to communicate with other fellow Logic users or when asking questions or engaging in discussions on various Logic forums.

The Visual Approach

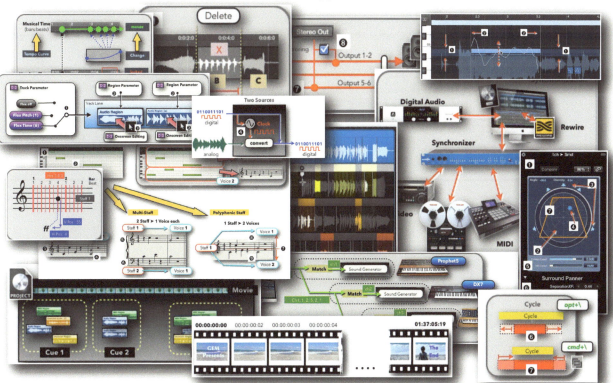

Here is a summary of the advantages of my Graphically Enhanced Manuals that set them apart from other books:

Better Learning	Better Value

☑ **Graphics, Graphics, Graphics**

Every feature and concept is explained with rich graphics and illustrations that are not found in any other book or User Guide, let alone YouTube videos. These are not just a few screenshots with arrows in it. I take the time to create unique diagrams to illustrate the concepts and workflows.

☑ **Knowledge and Understanding**

The purpose of my manuals is to provide the reader with the knowledge and understanding of an app that is much more valuable than just listing and explaining a set of features.

☑ **Comprehensive**

For any given feature, I list every available command so you can decide which one to use in your workflow. Some of the information is not even found in the app's User Guide.

☑ **For Beginners and Advanced Users**

The graphical approach makes my manuals easy to understand for beginners, but still, the wealth of information and details provide plenty of material, even for the most advanced user.

☑ **Three formats**

No other manual is available in all three formats: PDF (from my website), interactive multi-touch iBooks (on Apple's iBooks Store), and printed book (on Amazon).

☑ **Interactive iBooks**

No other manual is available in the enhanced iBooks format. I include an extensive glossary, also with additional graphics. Every term throughout the content of the iBook is linked to the glossary term that lets you pop up a little window with the explanations without leaving the page you are currently reading. Every term lists all the entries in the book where it is used and links to other related terms.

☑ **Free Updates** (pdf, iBook only)

No other manual provides free updates, I do. Whenever I update a book, I email a free download link to the pdf file to current customers. iBooks customers will receive an automatic update notification, and 24 hours after a new update, the printed book will be available on Amazon. They are print-on-demand books, which means, whenever you order a book on Amazon, you get the most recent version and not an outdated one that was sitting in a publisher's warehouse.

Self-published

As a self-published author, I can release my books without any restrictions imposed by a publisher. Rich, full-color graphics and interactive books are usually too expensive to produce for such a limited audience. However, I have read mountains of manuals throughout the 35 years of my professional career as a musician, composer, sound engineer, and teacher, and I am developing these Graphically Enhanced Manuals (GEM) based on that experience, the way I think a manual should be written. This is, as you can imagine, very time consuming and requires a lot of dedication.

However, not having a big publisher also means not having a big advertising budget and the connections to get my books into the available channels of libraries, bookstores, and schools. Instead, as a self-published author, I rely on reviews, blogs, referrals, and word of mouth to continue this series.
If you like my "Graphically Enhanced Manuals", you can help me promote these books by referring them to others and maybe taking a minute to write a review on Amazon or the iBooks Store.

Thanks, I appreciate it:

 http://amzn.to/1sP8jvl    http://bit.ly/1oJ7ftQ

Disclaimer: As a non-native English speaker, I try my best to write my manuals with proper grammar and spelling. However, not having a major publisher also means that I don't have a big staff of editors and proofreaders at my disposal. So, if something slips through and it really bothers you, email me at <GrammarPolice@DingDingMusic.com>, and I will fix it in the next update. Thanks!

LogicProGEM

Please check out my Logic site "LogicProGEM.com". The link "Blog" contains all the free Logic Articles that I have published on the web and continue to publish. These are in-depth tutorials that use the same concept of rich graphics to cover specific topics related to Logic Pro X.

Music Tech Explained - the visual approach

As additional educational material, I provide free instructional videos on my YouTube channel "Music Tech Explained - the visual approach".
These are high-quality videos in 4K about topics for Logic Pro X, Pro Tools, and general audio production workflow tips.

Don't forget to subscribe.

Highlights

Here is the list of highlights of the new Logic Pro X v10.4 features, displayed on the following window when you first open the app.

This page is only displayed the first time when you launch the new update of the Logic app, but there is a command in the Main Menu *Help ➤ What's New in Logic Pro* that lets you open that window again.

Minimum Requirement

Nothing has changed regarding the minimum requirement since Logic version 10.4.

To download this new Logic Pro X update v10.4.2, you have to have at least macOS 10.12 ("Sierra") installed on your computer. Any operating system before that, like OS X 10.11 ("El Capitan") or OS X 10.10 ("Yosemite"), is not compatible.

LPX v10.4.2

Compatibility:
macOS 10.12 or later, 64-bit processor

If you are still running El Capitan (10.11) or an earlier version, then you have to first upgrade to macOS 10.14)"Mojave"), macOS 10.13 ("High Sierra"), or at least macOS 10.12 ("Sierra") before you can install Logic Pro X 10.4.2. However, do your homework regarding the compatibility of the apps, plugins, and hardware you are using on your machine before making any OSX / macOS upgrade decision.

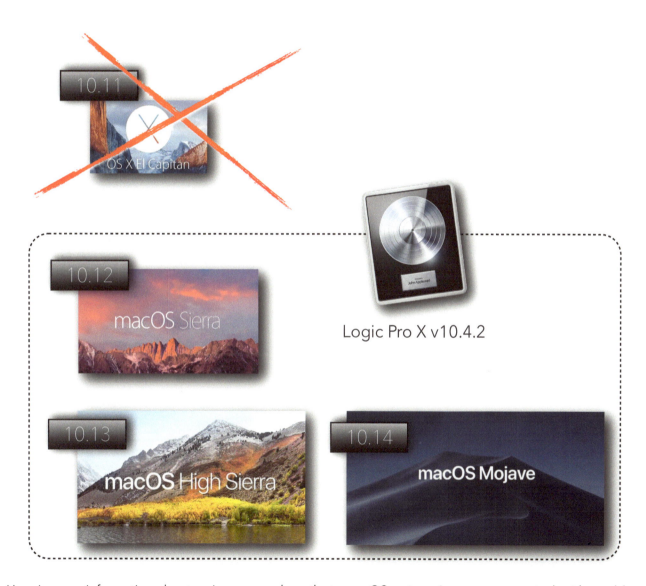

Logic Pro X v10.4.2

Here is some information about various upgrade paths to macOS systems in case you are stuck with an older computer that limits your options on what system it can run on it.

https://support.apple.com/en-us/HT206886

If you have an older MacPro that doesn't allow you to upgrade to at least macOS 10.12, google "*Mac Pro 2009-2010 Firmware Tool*" to find some "remedies".

Sound Library

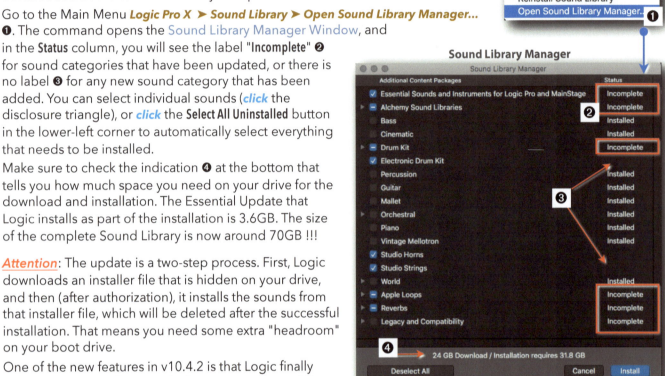

The Logic Pro v10.4.2 update doesn't add any new sounds to the Sound Library but check the following Sound Library window to make sure that you have downloaded all the sounds and they are up-to-date.

Go to the Main Menu *Logic Pro X ➤ Sound Library ➤ Open Sound Library Manager...* ❶. The command opens the Sound Library Manager Window, and in the **Status** column, you will see the label "**Incomplete**" ❷ for sound categories that have been updated, or there is no label ❸ for any new sound category that has been added. You can select individual sounds (*click* the disclosure triangle), or *click* the **Select All Uninstalled** button in the lower-left corner to automatically select everything that needs to be installed.

Make sure to check the indication ❹ at the bottom that tells you how much space you need on your drive for the download and installation. The Essential Update that Logic installs as part of the installation is 3.6GB. The size of the complete Sound Library is now around 70GB !!!

Attention: The update is a two-step process. First, Logic downloads an installer file that is hidden on your drive, and then (after authorization), it installs the sounds from that installer file, which will be deleted after the successful installation. That means you need some extra "headroom" on your boot drive.

One of the new features in v10.4.2 is that Logic finally allows you to save the Sound Library on an external drive.

➡ *Progress Bar*

During the download/installation pay attention to the LCD in the Logic Control Bar.

Control Bar (LCD)

- ▶ A blue line ❺ functions as a progress bar that moves from left to right, indicating the ongoing process.

- ▶ *Click* on the progress bar, and a popover ❻ appears with the information: what is downloaded, how much, and how long it takes until completion.

- ▶ The two buttons on the popover to the right ❼ let you either cancel ⊗ or pause ⏸ the process.

- ▶ If you pause a process, an orange bar ❽ appears below the LCD to indicate that.

- ▶ The Pause button ⏸ has changed to an orange Resume button ❾ 🔄 that, you guessed it, lets you resume the process when you *click* on it.

Bug Fixes

Every Logic user has their own "favorite" bug (depending on their workflow), waiting to be fixed. Here are a few ones on the list:

- ☑ No more unexpected quits or hangs when:
  - When importing project settings if it is connected to the Logic Remote app.
  - When analyzing surround files in the Smart Tempo Editor.
  - When recording from a surround input.
  - When performing Join per Track on a Summing Stack.
- ☑ Logic Pro now remains responsive when resizing the Key Commands window.
- ☑ The Open Movie file browser again remembers the last location used to open a movie file.
- ☑ When recording audio in **Replace** mode, the audio region is no longer cut short if there is also MIDI input during the recording, and the MIDI Replace mode is set to Region Punch.
- ☑ Punching in and out of record on an armed audio track with a MIDI track selected now creates a properly placed region with access to the pre-punch area of the recording.
- ☑ It is again possible to adjust the borders of multiple selected flexed regions.
- ☑ Setting a quantize value for a region with a **Flex & Follow** setting of **On + Align Bars & Beats** no longer resets the Flex & Follow setting to **On**.

The Logic Pro X v10.4.2 update comes with lots of bug fixes (read through the full Release Notes), but if your "favorite" bug is still not fixed, keep on reporting it to the official feedback page at
http://www.apple.com/feedback/logic-pro.html

Improvements

Besides the bug fixes, Logic updates usually include improvements regarding speed and responsiveness. Here are few important ones from the list:

- ☑ Reduced amount of memory consumed by ChromaVerb
- ☑ Improved accuracy of Loudness Meter.
- ☑ Logic Pro now always prompts for a Save when closing a Project that had been previously auto saved.
- ☑ Closing a newly created project before any changes have been made no longer triggers a Save dialog.
- ☑ Track color parameter to shown in control surfaces
- ☑ Added lookahead minimizes the artifacts in playback when using the Auto Voice Split feature in Studio Horns and Studio Strings.
- ☑ There is no longer a lag when selecting tracks in large projects.
- ☑ Performance when zooming in projects with a large number of Tempo events is improved.
- ☑ Logic Pro again remains fully responsive when starting a rubber band selection at a region border.
- ☑ There is no longer a lag when deleting multiple transient markers in the Smart Tempo Editor.
- ☑ Performance when moving beat markers in the Smart Tempo Editor is improved.
- ☑ Logic no longer sometimes starts to respond sluggishly after recalling screensets.
- ☑ New sample rates offered when changing audio hardware in Logic Pro preferences are now immediately available.
- ☑ Bouncing a looped region in place now includes the loops as well as the original region.

3 - Big New Features

Sound Library Relocation

Finally, this is a feature that Logic users have waited for a long time, and here is why:

▶ **Pro**: Logic Pro X is great because it comes with a huge amount of free content, over 70GB of samples, loops, instruments and various sound files, Logic's so-called Sound Library.

▶ **Con**: All those files have to be installed on your local Boot Drive, which can cause a problem if you are running out of space on that drive.

▶ **Unofficial Fix**: In the past, you could move those files to a separate drive and use an Alias in the Finder to link to them. However, this doesn't work anymore with Logic Pro X and requires a more complicated fix, using Symbolic Links (some Unix trickery).

▶ **Official Fix**: Logic Pro X v10.4.2 now offers a built-in easy-to-use feature to move the Logic Sound Library to a different drive, freeing up space on your boot drive (basically using the same Unix trickery with a simple user interface).

Basics

Relocating the Logic Sound Library now is as easy as three clicks. However, there are a lot of little details that I think you should know about. There is always something that could go wrong and it is not a bad idea to understand the underlying architecture a little better in case you have to straighten out some mishaps.

Let's start with a few basics about Logic's Sound Library.

➡ *Sound Library (Factory Sounds)*

The Sound Library are factory sounds, which means they come from Apple, included with Logic Pro X. They are broken up into two parts:

● **Essential Sounds**: When you install Logic the first time, then part of the installation procedure is the download and installation of the Essential Sounds of the Sound Library. These are sound files, using about 2GB of disk space, for main instruments and sounds to get you started.

● **Additional Content**: In addition to the Essential Sounds, you can pick and choose later which part of the entire Sound Library, the Additional Content, you want to download based on what specific content you need or how much space you have available.

Because the Sound Library are factory sounds, there are a few things you have to be aware of in general, and also things to know when it comes to relocating those files:

☑ Deleting the Sound Library (on purpose or by accident) is not a big deal because those files can always be re-downloaded from inside Logic.

☑ The Save Project Dialog ❶ lets you choose ❷ whether you want to save Sound Library files with your Project File if you use any of those files in your Project.

☑ Because these are factory sounds, they are not stored in your User Directory. They are located in the System Library Directory on the root level of your Boot Drive (*/Library/*).

☑ The new Relocate Sound Library feature now lets you move those files to a different drive.

➡️ Location

The Sound Library is not just one single folder with sound files. Instead, it represents many different types of files that are stored in different locations. This is where it gets already a bit complicated. In addition, the new Relocate Sound Library feature doesn't affect the entire Sound Library. You have to know which one it affects (and which one not) so you understand what files (from which location) are actually moved.

Here are the three main locations where the files of the Logic Sound Library are stored by default:

🟡 /Library /Audio/

These are two types of audio files, Apple Loops and Impulse Responses (which together add up to a little bit under 10GB). And here is already the first restriction regarding the Relocate Sound Library feature. Those files cannot be relocated!

/Library/Audio/

- ☑️ **Apple Loops**: These are the Apple Loops that are displayed in Logic's Loop Browser together with the Apple Loops you created yourself.
- ☑️ **Impulse Responses**: The so-called Impulse Responses are short audio files that are the foundation for so-called "Convolution Reverbs". Logic's Space Designer is one of those convolution reverbs and these are the files that the Plugin uses for its presets.

🟡 /Library/Application Support/Logic/

This is the main location that stores most of the Sound Library, but also contains files that are not considered part of the Sound Library (especially some obsolete files from earlier Logic installations). Regardless of what these files are, this is the folder that is moved with all its content when using the Relocate command.

/Library/Application Support/Logic/

- ☑️ **Alchemy Samples**: These are all the samples that are used by the Alchemy Plugin.
- ☑️ **Ultrabeat Samples**: These are all the samples that are used by the Ultrabeat Plugin.
- ☑️ **EXS Factory Samples**: These are all the samples that are used by the EXS24 Plugin. Please note that this folder also includes all the samples for the Drum Kit Designer, the Studio Horns, and Studio Strings because they are technically EXS Instruments (on steroids).
- ☑️ **Sampler Instruments**: These are all the EXS Sampler Instruments (**.exs**) that are used by the EXS24 Plugin. Please note that this folder also includes all the EXS Sampler Instruments for the Drum Kit Designer, the Studio Horns, and Studio Strings because, technically, they are all EXS Instruments.
- ☑️ **Settings**: The Sound Library does not only include audio files (loops, samples, etc.) but also various types of presets. They are also located in this directory in various subfolder (**Patches**, **Plug-In Settings**). However, most of those settings are now embedded inside the Logic app, and the corresponding folders you see in this directory are obsolete (if you don't use older Logic apps that rely on them).
- ☑️ **"Others"**: There are also other types of files stored in this directory (i.e., Key Commands, Chord Grids, Templates, etc.). No matter if they are legacy files, they are all moved with the Logic folder when using the Relocate command.

🟡 "Embedded" Settings Files

Here are some of the file types that are "embedded" in the Logic app. If you know how to "open" the Logic bundle, then you can find them in the **Resources** directory. Again, if you see any of those folders in the Logic folder (**/Library/Application Support/Logic/**), then they are obsolete and not used by the current Logic app (v10.4.2) anymore and, instead, Logic uses its embedded files. Either delete them (if you are sure about it) or let them drag along when you use the Relocate command (they are not that big).

- ☑️ Patches
- ☑️ Plug-In Settings
- ☑️ Project Templates
- ☑️ Key Commands
- ☑️ Chord Grids

Sound Library Manager

The menu command *Logic Pro X* ➤ *Sound Library...* ❶ opens a submenu with all the commands related to the Sound Library, including the command **Open Sound Library Manager...** ❷ that opens the Sound Library Manager ❸. It lists all the available content and lets you choose which one to download.

Sound Library Manager

 **Relocate**

Here is the concept behind relocating the Sound Library.

● Default Location

As we have seen, the default location of the Sound Library ❹ is on the same System Drive ❺ (the Boot Drive) where Logic ❻ is installed on.

Logic is "linked" to that Sound Library.

● Moved Location

With the new Relocate Sound Library feature, you will be able to move ("relocate") the Sound Library to any other (eligible) drive (let's call it "External Drive" ❼) so Logic ❽ will be linked ❾ to the Sound Library in that location.

Please note that this link functions in both directions.

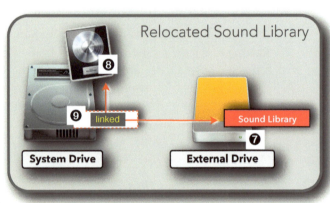

- ☑ **Access Sound Library**: When you access any Sound Library content (EXS Instruments, Drummers, Alchemy Instruments, etc.) in your Logic Project, it loads those files from that Sound Library location ❼.

- ☑ **Install new Sound Library**: Whenever you install new Sound Library content using the Sound Library Manager ❸, Logic would store those new files in the System Library ❹ by default. However, when the Sound Library has been moved to a different location, then all the new content will be installed directly in that location ❼ and not on the System Drive.

Relocated Sound Library

➤ **Space Considerations**

Moving the Sound Library to an "External Drive" has the advantage that when you install Logic on a new computer, you only need about 2GB space on the Boot Drive for the Essential Sounds of the Sound Library. Before you install the 70GB of Additional Content, you relocate the Sound Library first to an "External Drive" ❼ so all that content will now be installed directly on that "External Drive". You still need the up to 10GB space for the Apple Loops and Impulse Responses that remain on the Boot Drive.

- Keep in mind that the installation procedure happens in smaller steps. Each step downloads an installer file (containing the sound files) to a hidden location on your Boot Drive and then installs those files to their final destination. The installer file is then deleted and the next section is downloaded. That means you still need some space on your Boot Drive for those temporary installer files.

Relocate Procedure

Here is the step-by-step procedure on how to relocate the Sound Library:

⬤ Step 1: Open the Relocate Sound Library Dialog

Use the command from the Main Menu *Logic Pro X* ➤ *Sound Library* ➤ *Relocate Sound Library...* ❶ to open the Relocate Sound Library Dialog ❷

Here is what you see:

▶ **Header**: The text ❸ on top shows you how big your current Sound Library is so you know how much space you need.

▶ **List of Drives**: The list ❹ displays each mounted drive on your computer as a separate row.

▶ **Columns**: The list has three columns:

- **Location**: This is the name of the drive.
- **Free Space**: This is the amount of free space on that drive.
- **Status**: An empty field indicates that this drive is available as a destination. If not, then the field lists the reason why not and the row is gray.

Relocate Sound Library Dialog

⬤ Step 2: Select the Destination Drive

You *click* on the row ❺ of the drive that you choose as the destination where you want to move the Sound Library to. The row is now highlighted and the **Relocate** ❻ button in the lower-right corner turns blue, ready to relocate.

⬤ Step 3: Relocate

Click on the **Relocate** ❻ button to start the process. A progress bar ❼ and a numeric indication ❽ appears at the bottom of the dialog to indicate the progress.

The Relocate Sound Library Dialog will close once the process is completed and a new dialog pops up to confirm that ❾.

⬤ Step 4 (optional): Relocate Back to Boot Drive

Now, when you open the Relocate Sound Library Dialog again, you will see that the **Status** ❿ field of the drive you moved the Sound Library to indicates "**Current Sound Library files location**". The **Status** field of the Boot Drive is now empty, which means you could move the Sound Library back to it by selecting that row and repeat Step 2 and 3.

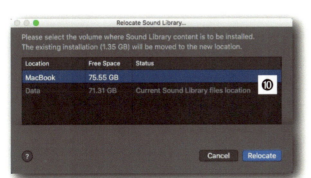

The following pages are for Logic users who want to have a better understanding of the Relocate Sound Library feature and want to know what happens behind the scene. Plus, there are some compatibility considerations.

➡️ *Finder*

Here is a look at what happens on the Finder level when you relocate the Sound Library:

🟡 *Boot Drive - Before*

This is a screenshot of the System Library ❶.

▶ **Logic folder ❷**:
/Library/Application Support/Logic/ The **Logic** folder contains the Sound Library that we want to relocate (move).

▶ **GarageBand folder ❸**:
/Library/Application Support/GarageBand/ Please be aware that the Relocate procedure also moves this **GarageBand** folder.

▶ **Audio folder ❹**
/Library/Audio/ Remember, the content of the **Audio** folder (Apple Loops and Impulse Responses) will not be moved.

🟡 *Boot Drive - After*

The **Logic** ❺ folder and the **GarageBand** ❻ folder are each replaced by an Alias Folder (indicated by the

arrow on their folder icon ↗), and as you can see, the **Audio** folder has not changed.

🟡 *Destination Drive*

This is the screenshot of the External Drive "Data" ❼.

Logic creates a new folder **Library** on the root level of that drive that contains a subfolder **Application Support**. They contain the two original folders **Logic** ❽ and **GarageBand** ❾ that were moved from the Boot Drive ❷ ❸ containing the sound files. Logic is now linked to those folders.

🟡 *Destination Drive (Relocate)*

If you would relocate the Sound Library back to the Boot Drive, then those two folders **Logic** and **GarageBand** would be moved back ❷ ❸, but the now empty **Library** and **Application Support** folders ❿ remain on that drive.

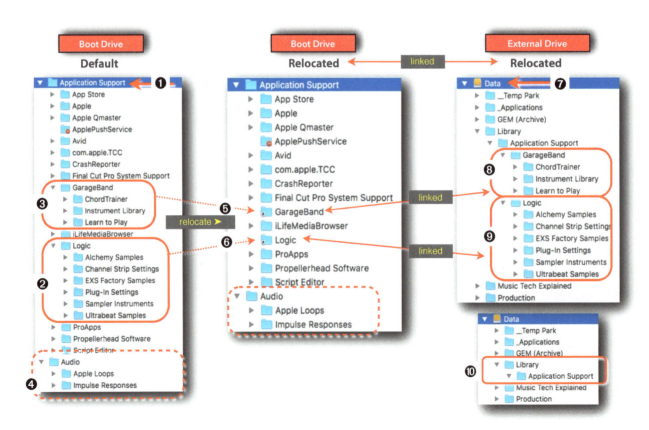

Symlink

The Alias Folders on the Boot Drive that appear after the Relocate procedure look like standard Aliases, the ones you can create in the Finder, indicated by the icon with the little arrow ❶. However, they are a so-called Symlinks (Symbolic Links), which you can verify when you view the files ❷ in the Terminal app.

Similar to an Alias, a Symlink file contains the path ❸ to the location (Volume and Folder) where the actual file or folder, in this case, the Sound Library, is stored.

```
                                          Terminal
urwxrwxrwx  11 root   admin    374       2017 Avid
drwxrwxr-x   9 root   admin    306      11:27 CrashReporter
drwxrwxr-x   3 root   admin    102  ❷   2017 Final Cut Pro System Support
lrwxr-xr-x   1 root   admin     52      16:17 GarageBand -> /Volumes/Data/Library/Application Support/GarageBand
lrwxr-xr-x   1 root   admin     47      16:17 Logic -> /Volumes/Data/Library/Application Support/Logic
drwxrwxr-t   3 root   admin    102       2017 ProApps                                          ❸
drwxrwxrwx   3 root   admin    102       2017 Propellerhead Software
```

 Restrictions

Please keep in mind that there are a few restrictions.

🟡 Destination Drive - Root Level

The Sound Library can only be moved to the root level of a Destination Drive. You cannot select a specific folder or subfolder where you want to store the Sound Library to. That's why the Relocate Sound Library Dialog only lists the name ❹ of all the available drives in the **Location** field, and you cannot navigate to any other location on that drive.

🟡 Volume Status

Only the volumes with no entry ❺ in the **Status** field are available to move the Sound Library to. If the **Status** field has an entry, then that text explains why that drive is not available as a destination and the row is grayed out. Here are a few reasons why:

Relocate Sound Library Dialog

Location	Free Space	Status
SSD_5k ❹	681.02 GB	Current Sound Library files location
TimeMachine	493.06 GB	Time Machine backup drive
HighSierra 1TB	954.57 GB	Sound Library files exist here
Data	72.59 GB	Not enough free space
Drobo-1	10.2 TB	← ❺
edgar	74.2 GB	Incompatible file system
2018-06-26_11-52-54	479.1 MB	Do not have access rights

- **Current Sound Library files location**: This is the drive with the Sound Library that Logic is currently linked to.
- **Sound Library files exit here**: This is a drive that contains a Sound Library that Logic is currently not linked to. This can be either a System Drive that has Logic installed on it or a drive that you have once moved the Sound Library to and now contain the folder path */Library/Application Support/Logic/*.
- **Time Machine backup drive**: You cannot move the Sound Library to a drive that is used by TimeMachine.
- **Do not have access rights**: Read-only volumes cannot be used as a Destination Drive.
- **Incompatible file system**: Network Drives cannot be used as Destination Drives, indicated by this message.
- **Not enough free space**: This is a drive that you allowed to move the Sound Library to, but unfortunately, it doesn't have enough space.

 Relocate Logic + GarageBand

The Relocate procedure moves the Sound Library not only for the Logic sounds but also for the GarageBand sounds as I showed on the previous screenshots of the Finder. The Relocate Sound Library Dialog doesn't indicate that in any way.

GarageBand and previous Logic versions don't know the new Relocate feature, which could cause problems under some circumstances. I will show that in the next few pages.

➡️ *Drive Note Mounted*

The advantage of having the Sound Library stored on the Boot Drive is that it is always available when you work in Logic. However, once you relocate (move) the Sound Library to a different drive, then you could run into an issue when that drive is not available (volume not mounted). What happens in that case depends on different circumstances with different outcomes.

Whenever you launch Logic, it always verifies the existence of the Sound Library. If the Sound Library cannot be found at the location the Symlink File tells it to (because the drive is not mounted), then a dialog ❶ pops up with three options.

🟡 *Retry*

If you realize that you forgot to mount the drive that contains the Sound Library, then you just mount it and click the **Retry** ❷ button. Logic will now be able to link to the Sound Library and launches properly. The text ❷ in the dialog even tells you the name of the drive Logic is looking for.

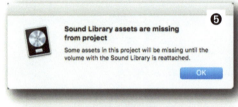

🟡 *Ignore*

Clicking the **Ignore** ❹ button will continue to launch Logic, but another dialog ❺ pops up to warn you about the situation you are getting into. Your Project might not play back properly.

For example, the Library Browser still shows Patches, but they are grayed out ❻, or the New Tracks Dialog ❼ doesn't show the Drummer icon because it can't find the files on the Sound Library for the Drummers.

🟡 *Reset*

Be careful with this **Reset** ❽ option. A Warning Dialog ❾ pops up telling you that the Reset command will **"break the link"** (removes the Symlink file) to the drive that is currently storing the System Library.

Here is what happens when you click the **Reset** button:

- ☑️ Logic will start to download the Essential Sounds.
- ☑️ A window ❿ opens that shows you the progress of the download. This is the same window that you see when you install Logic the first time.
- ☑️ Once the download is completed, a window pops up where you have to authenticate your user account to authorize Logic so it can place the Sound Library in the System Library Folder.
- ☑️ Logic is now again linked to the (newly downloaded) Sound Library on the Boot Drive in its default location ***/Library/Application Support/Logic/***.
- ☑️ The previous Symlink File **Logic** is removed from the System Library Folder.

Warning

If you use the **Reset** command, then Logic only installs the Essential Sounds (2GB). If you had previously installed and relocated the entire 70GB Sound Library to a separate drive, then you have to download and re-install the entire 70GB again. Not recommended if you live out there in the woods still with an AOL dial-up account.

➡️ *After Reset*

Please note that the previous Reset procedure does not remove the Sound Library (all the files) on the External Drive (which is currently not mounted anyways). When you later mount that drive and open the Relocate Sound Library Dialog ❶ in Logic, you will see in the **Status** field "**Sound Library files exist here**" ❷. You cannot re-link to that drive. You would have to manually delete that Library folder in that location and redo the entire Relocate procedure again.

Relocate Sound Library Dialog

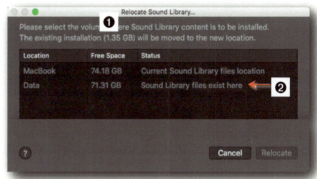

➡️ *Incompatibility and Precaution*

Using the new Relocate feature with the new Logic Pro X version 10.4.2 works great. However, if you relocated the Sound Library and then launch a previous Logic version or launch GarageBand, what will happen? Those apps don't know anything about a Relocate feature. Here are three scenarios you have to be aware of:

🟡 *Scenario 1: Proper Functionality*

This is the situation where the External Drive that contains the Sound Library is mounted and the Alias File is located in the System Folder pointing at that drive.

The good news is that any older Logic app or the GarageBand app would properly link to the relocated Sound Library because the Relocate feature is not some new trick introduced in Logic Pro X 10.4.2. It just relies on Symlinks, which is a standard macOS "redirect functionality" that works with other apps too.

🟡 *Scenario 2: Drive not mounted*

This is the situation where the External Drive with the Sound Library that Logic is linked to is not mounted.

- ▸ **Logic 10.4.2**: The dialog ❸ with the three options pops up again that I explained on the previous page (**Reset**, **Ignore**, **Retry**).
- ▸ **Older Logic apps**: If it can't link to a valid Sound Library, then it opens the download window ❹ and re-installs the Sound Library on the Boot Drive and deletes the **Logic** Alias Folder!)
- ▸ **GarageBand app**: If it can't link to a valid Sound Library, then it opens the download window ❹ and re-installs the Sound Library on the Boot Drive. Please note that GarageBand creates a new **GarageBand** folder (*/Library/ Application Support/GarageBand/* and also a new **Logic** folder (*/Library/Application Support/Logic/*) on the Boot Drive with the Essential Sounds needed for GarageBand to run. This also deletes the **Logic** and **GarageBand** Alias Folders!

🟡 *Scenario 3: Alias File is missing*

In this situation, the Alias Folders that are pointing at the drive containing the Sound Library have been deleted by accident or were deleted by the re-installation procedure (Scenario 2).

- ▸ **Logic 10.4.2**: Logic will re-create that **Logic** Alias Folder, places it in the System Library Folder so it can properly link to the Sound Library on the External Drive (if it is mounted).
- ▸ **Older Logic apps**: Same as scenario 2, installs new Sound Library on the Boot Drive.
- ▸ **GarageBand app**: Same as scenario 2, installs new Sound Library on the Boot Drive.

➡️ *Fixing the Mess*

If a re-installation of the Sound Library deletes the existing Alias Folders (because the External Drive was not mounted), then you end up with a problem.

When you relocate the Sound Library, Logic is doing something behind the scene. It will not only store a note (somewhere?) that you have relocated the Sound Library, it also saves the actual path to the new location. This is the reason why Logic still can link to the Sound Library on an External Drive, even if the Alias Folder was deleted (Scenario 2).

But here is a special situation that you could run into:

- ▶ As we have seen in Scenario 2 and Scenario 3, it could happen that an older Logic version or GarageBand will re-install the Sound Library on the Boot Drive.
- ▶ Any time the Sound Library is installed, it will delete any existing **Logic** or **GarageBand** Alias File.
- ▶ If you would now launch Logic Pro X 10.4.2 it would face a conflict:
  - ☑ Logic remembers the note that it had relocated the Sound Library to an External Drive.
  - ☑ It would expect to see the Alias File (*/Library/Application Support/Logic"Alias"*), but it is not there.
  - ☑ As we have seen in Scenario 3, Logic would just recreate the Alias File, but it doesn't do that because it sees a valid Sound Library in the System Library folder (*/Library/Application Support/Logic/*).
  - ☑ Based on that conflict, Logic opens a dialog ❶ that lets you resolve that conflict by choosing one of the two options.

- • **Link ❷**: Logic deletes the two folders **Logic** and **GarageBand** on the Boot Drive (*/Library/Application Support/*) that contain the Sound Library and recreates the two Alias Folders **Logic** and **GarageBand** that point to the Drive it had previously relocated the Sound Library to. The Alert window even lists the name ❸ of that Drive ("Data") in the text.
- • **Keep ❹**: Logic updates its information (that is was linked to the Sound Library on an External Drive) so it now links to the Sound Library on the Boot Drive. The Sound Library (the files) on the External Drive remains on that drive and will not be deleted. Unfortunately, you cannot relink to that Sound Library later on. If you want to use that External Drive, you would have to delete the Library folder on the root level of that drive (or rename it) and use the Relocate procedure again.

➡️ *Drive Terminology*

Because using Logic's Relocate feature involves drives, here is a list of terms that describe various drives and their functionality, some geek stuff you should be familiar with.

- ▶ **System Drive**: A System Drive is a drive that has a macOS system installed on it.
- ▶ **Boot Drive**: If you boot from a System Drive, it becomes the Boot Drive.
- ▶ **Internal Drive**: An Internal Drive is a hard drive installed inside your computer.
- ▶ **External Drive**: An External Drive is a drive connected to your computer (even a USB stick) through one of its ports (USB, Thunderbolt, etc.).
- ▶ **Network Drive**: A Network Drive is a drive mounted on a different computer and connected (and mounted) to the local computer over a network (Ethernet).

- ▶ **Cloud Drive**: A Cloud Drive is also a Network Drive, but connected wirelessly over the Internet.
- ▶ **Partition**: You can divide the total amount of storage space on a drive into so-called Partitions, each one functions as an individual drive.
- ▶ **Disk Image**: A Disk Image is a special folder that can be mounted like a drive.
- ▶ **Volume**: The term "Volume" is used in computers for any logical storage unit, no matter if it is a single drive or a partition of a drive.

Introduction

Logic Pro X 10.4.2 has a new Mixer Mode called "**Sends on Faders**". However, the new Mixer Mode contains two components, "Sends on Fader" and "**Independent Pan**". They provide a much better flexibility and better workflow when using Sends in your mixer setup.

Although the feature itself is great, I'm not really thrilled about its implementation. I don't find it that intuitive and even partially confusing how the various commands are laid out and labeled. But hey, that's what a manual is for to explain how it works. And after all, there is always an update after the current update, and maybe it will improve in the future or perhaps it is only me and the majority of Logic users don't have an issue with that. Let's get into it and judge for yourself.

 Two Components

As I already mentioned, the new Mixer Mode provides two new functionalities. Here is a short description:

🟡 Sends on Faders

When using Sends in your Mixer setup, you can route the signal on a Channel Strip to one of the 256 Busses. The Send Level Knob ❶ lets you control the level on how much you want to send to the selected Bus.

The new Sends on Faders functions like a switch that lets you temporarily change the mixer view so you can use the Volume Fader to control the send level which provides a more comfortable and precise level adjustment

There is a new popup menu ❷ in the Mixer that lets you select one of the current Aux Returns (and the Bus used on that return) and now only the Channel Strips that have a Send to that selected Bus (those Send Slots turns yellow ❸) have a Volume Fader that now functions as the Sends Level. Those special Volume Faders are now also marked with a yellow Fader Knob ❹).

🟡 Pan Sends

Logic doesn't have a dedicated Pan Sends, a Pan Control on the Sends (a long-standing omission). You can only set the level ❶ that you want to send to a bus, but if you send a stereo or multi-channel signal to the bus, you have no way to change the pan on that signal. The only way was to use the "Post Pan" option to tap the signal after the Channel Strip's Pan Control.

Now, Logic lets you add a dedicated Pan Control to the Sends signal, a feature called "Independent Pan". It uses the Pan Control ❻ on the Channel Strip, which is now marked yellow This is not a global command. You can select on which Channel Strip and which Send Slot but is only displayed when Sends on Faders ❼ is selected. And there are a few more conditions that you have to be aware of.

Sends on Faders

The new Mixer Mode requires that you have a proper understanding of signal routing in Logic, which is similar to most DAWs that follow the concept of a traditional mixing console. I will provide some signal flow diagrams in this section to better demonstrate the functionality and, hopefully, that will help to understand this new feature better.

➡️ *Signal Routing*

Let's start with a review of the basic concepts of Busses, Sends, and Returns.

▶ **Bus**: Logic has 256 Busses ❶. They act like pipes where you can send audio signals to (from a Channel Strip) and also tap into those pipes and return the sum of all audio signals on a specific bus (back to a Channel Strip). The Mixer architecture (based on the concept of traditional mixing consoles) has other types of busses like the Input Busses (signal coming from your Audio Interface) and Output Busses (signals sent to the Audio Interface). To avoid confusion with those Input Busses and Output Busses, theses "Busses" here are also referred to as Auxiliary Busses (not to be confused with Aux Returns, see below) or Internal Busses because the audio signal is routed on those busses only inside the Mixer and is not connected to any external Audio Interface.

▶ **Sends**: You can route the audio signal on most Channel Strips to those Busses (in addition to routing the signal to the Channel Strip's Output). This is referred to as the "Sends" ❷, a specific component on a Channel Strip.

▶ **Send Slots**: Logic Pro X has 8 Send Slots ❸ so you can send the audio signal on a Channel Strip to up to eight different Busses that you select on each Send Slot.

▶ **Return**: You can route ("Return" ❹) a specific bus back to a Channel Strip so that Channel Strip receives all the signals that are sent to that Bus. An Aux Channel Strip is commonly used for that purpose, and that's why that Channel Strip Type is also referred to as the "Aux Return".

▶ **Input Selector**: In Logic Pro X, only the Aux Channel Strip and the Audio Channel Strip have the option in their Input Selector ❺ to choose one of the 256 Busses as their input as a "Return".

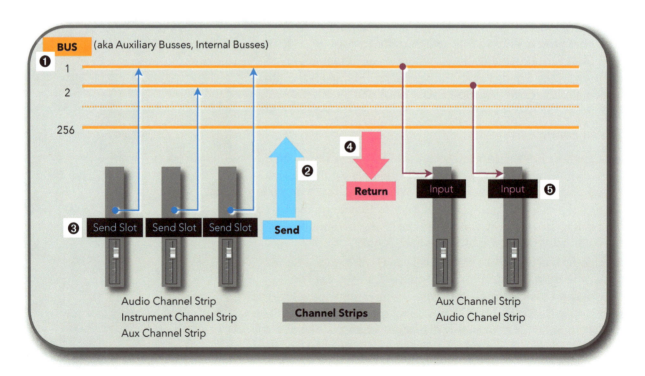

➡️ **What's Different?**

First, let's explore the interface to see what is different before explaining what those changes mean and how to use them.

🟡 *Sends on Faders Controls*

The first thing we will notice when opening the Mixer Window is that section ❶ on top next to the three local menus. There are three elements:

Mixer Window ❶

▸ **Label ❷**: The label "**Sends on Faders:**" tells you what the two new controls are for.
▸ **On/Off Button** ⏻ ⏻ ❸: The button toggles the Sends on Faders View on/off. Please note that Sends on Faders is only a display function and has no effect on your audio signals when switching.
▸ **Selector ❹**: The selector opens a dynamic popup menu when you *click* on it that lists all the "Returns", which are Aux Channel Strips and Audio Channel Strips that use a Bus as their input. Please check the diagram on the previous page.

If you have no "Aux Returns" in your Mixer, then the popup menu can't be opened (there is nothing on it) and the On/Off Button can't be turned on.

🟡 *Sends Menu*

When you *click* on an empty Send Slot ❺, then the menu that opens only provides the **Bus** submenu that lets you select one of the 256 Busses to route that Send to.

When you *click* on a Send Slot that is already assigned to a Bus ❼, then the menu has four more options in addition to the three options **Post Pan**, **Post Fader**, **Pre Fader**).

• **Independent Pan ❽**: Selecting this option will add a dedicated Pan Control to that Send. More about that Send Pan in a moment.
• **Copy Fader to Send ❾**: This command uses the value of the Channel Strip's Volume Fader (i.e., **-9dB**) and sets the Send Level to that value (i.e., **-9dB**).
• **Copy Pan to Send ❿**: This command uses the value of the Channel Strip's Pan Control and sets the Send Pan to that value. The command is grayed out if the Send doesn't have a dedicated Pan Control (the **Independent Pan ❽** option if not enabled)
• **Sends on Faders ⓫**: *Click* on this option and Sends on Faders selects the Return that uses this Bus. *Click* on it if the option is selected to turn Sends on Faders off.

➡️ **Sends on Faders**

Here is an example to demonstrate the functionality of the new Sends on Faders feature.

🟡 Channel Strips

I have a Mixer setup with 6 Audio Channel Strips ❶:

- ☑️ On every Channel Strip, I use Sends ❷, one or two. Those Send Slots are blue, and their label displays the Bus number I selected on that Send Slot. If you assigned custom labels in the I/O Label Window, then you would see those labels instead.
- ☑️ You can choose any Bus number, and I purposely didn't use **Bus 1**, **Bus 2**, and **Bus 3** to avoid any false assumption with the name/numbering of the Aux Channel Strips. I chose **Bus 5**, **Bus 7**, and **Bus 9**.

🟡 Aux Channel Strips

Look at the Aux Channel Strips ❸ on the right:

- ☑️ Please note that every time you select a Bus on a Send Slot of a Channel Strip, Logic will automatically create an Aux Channel Strip and sets its input to receive that Bus.
- ☑️ These three Aux Channel Strips in the Mixer were created by Logic based on that functionality and as you can see on their Input Selector ❹, they are set to receive **Bus 5**, **Bus 7**, and **Bus 9**.
- ☑️ These three Aux Channel Strips are the so-called "Returns" in my mixer setup.

🟡 Sends on Faders Menu - Returns

Here is what we see in the Sends on Faders Menu when *clicking* on the Sends on Faders Selector ❻:

- ☑️ The menu has three entries in my mixer setup.
- ☑️ Each entry represents a "Return", the Aux Channel Strip that uses a Bus as its input.
- ☑️ The label shows the Bus number ❼ (the Bus selected on the Input of that Return) and the name of the Aux Channel Strip ❽ (the Return) it is routed to.

Please note that, instead of an Aux Channel Strip, you can also use an Audio Channel Strip as the Return by selecting that specific bus as the input of the Audio Channel Strip. Or you can select the same Bus as the input on more than one Aux or Audio Channel Strip to create multiple Returns. However, this new feature seems to be a little bit buggy regarding on what is displayed in the popup menu in those cases ❺.

One more word of caution. Please don't confuse a Bus (Auxiliary Bus) with an Aux Channel Strip. These are two different components.

➡️ **User Interface**

Here is what happens when you select an option from the Sends on Faders Menu:

- ☑️ All the Volume Faders on the Aux Channel Strips disappear ❶ with the exception of the Aux Channel Strip ❷ that you selected from the menu (the Return).
- ☑️ All the Volume Faders disappear ❹ on the other Channel Strips with the exception of the Channel Strips that have a Send assigned to the Bus that is feeding the selected Aux Channel Strip (the Return).
- ☑️ Those "remaining" Volume Faders have a yellow Fader Knob ❺ to indicate that they now control a Send Level.
- ☑️ A Send Slot ❻ that changes to yellow indicates that this Send (Bus) is controlled by the yellow Volume Fader ❺ on the Channel Strip.
- ☑️ The Send Level Knobs on yellow Sends Slots are still active. That means you can adjust the Send Level with that knob ❻ or the yellow Volume Fader ❺.
- ☑️ The Level Meter next to the Volume Fader doesn't switch!

In the three screenshots, each one has a different Return selected in the Sends on Faders Menu ❸.

🟡 **Example 1**

The selected Return is the Aux Channel Strip "**Aux 1**" ❷. Its Volume Fader is still visible.

Bus 5 is feeding this Return, so all the Channel Strips that use a Send to Bus 5 have a yellow Volume Fader, and the Send Slots **Bus 5** turn yellow.

🟡 **Example 2**

The selected Return is the Aux Channel Strip "**Aux 2**"❼. Its Volume Fader is still visible.

Bus 7 is feeding this Return, so the two Channel Strips ❽ that use a Send to Bus 7 have a yellow Volume Fader, and the Send Slots **Bus 7** turn yellow.

🟡 **Example 3**

The selected Return is the Aux Channel Strip "**Aux 3**" ❾. Its Volume Fader is still visible.

Bus 9 is feeding this Return, so only one Channel Strip ❿ that uses a Send to Bus 9 has a yellow Volume Fader, and the Send Slot **Bus 9** turns yellow.

In case you haven't noticed, all the Pan Controls on the Channel Strips disappeared in the Sends on Faders View. We will find out in a moment why.

➡️ Select Sends on Faders

There are four options on how to toggle or select a Return for Sends on Faders.

🟡 Sends on Faders Menu

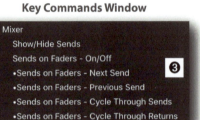

Mixer: Sends on Faders Control

▶ **Toggle**: *Clicking* on the On/Off Button ⏻ ⏻ ❶ toggles the Sends on Faders View. Turning it on will select the Return that was selected last.

▶ **Select**: Select an item from the menu ❷ to switch the Mixer view to that Return. Sends be enabled if it was off.

🟡 Key Commands

There are five new Key Commands ❸ for Sends on Faders (that are not assigned to any Key Equivalent by default). Make sure the Mixer Window has key focus when using them.

Key Commands Window

▶ **Sends on Faders - On/Off**: This has the same functionality as *clicking* the On/Off Button ⏻ ⏻.

▶ **Sends on Faders - Next Send**: Cycles through (forward) all Sends used on all currently selected Channel Strips and, therefore, selecting the Return that uses that Bus on its Input.

▶ **Sends on Faders - Previous Send**: Cycles through (backward) all Sends used on all currently selected Channel Strips and, therefore, selecting the Return that uses that Bus on its Input.

▶ **Sends on Faders - Cycle Through Sends**: Same as "Next Sends" but this time the cycle included the **Off** status

▶ **Sends on Faders - Cycle Through Returns**: Cycles through the options (including off) in the Sends on Faders Menu.

🟡 Sends Menu

Clicking on a Send Slot ❹ opens the Sends Menu ❺ that has the option Sends on Faders ❻ at the bottom.

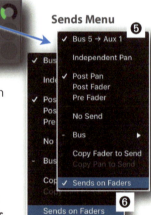

Sends Menu

☑ If the option is not selected, then it means that Sends on Faders is either off or selected on a Return that uses a different Bus. *Click* on the option and Sends on Faders selects the Return that uses this Bus

☑ If the option is selected, then it means that the Return that uses this Bus is selected. *Click* on it to turn Sends on Faders off.

🟡 Channel Strip Shortcut Menu

*Right-clic*k on the background ❼ of an Aux Channel Strip (or an Audio Channel Strip that has a Bus selected as its input) to open the Shortcut Menu that also lists the **Sends on Faders** ❽ option at the bottom. Be careful; the functionality is different from the option in the previous menu.

☑ If the option is not selected, then it means that Sends on Faders is off. *Click* on the option to turn it on with this Channel Strip selected as the Return.

☑ If the option is enabled, then it means that Sends on Faders is enabled. If you *click* on the option then the Sends on Faders is set to the Return of this Channel Strip if it wasn't the one that was currently selected. This is really a strange implementation of a menu item.

Channel Strip Shortcut Menu

Please Note: The Aux Channel Strips of a Summing Stack are only displayed in the Sends on Faders Menu if it is expanded (made visible in the Mixer Window).

Send Pan

First, the good news:

> **You can add a Pan Control to a Send**

Now, the not so good news:

> *The implementation is a little bit un-elegant.*

Here is a run-down:

- ☑ You add a Pan Control to a Send by enabling the menu item **Independent Pan** ❶ in the Sends Menu of that specific Send Slot ❷
- ☑ If you would expect a Pan Control to appear, you will be disappointed, because it doesn't.
- ☑ At least, the color ring around the Send Level Knob that indicates the Send Level changes to yellow ❸, which tells you that this Send has an additional Send Pan
- ☑ In order to see the Send Pan and make adjustments, you have to enable the Sends on Faders View ❺, which I would not have expected.
- ☑ However, just *clicking* on the Sends on Faders On/Off Button ❺ [icon] [icon] on the Mixer Window wouldn't do it, you also have to make sure to select the corresponding Return ❻ that uses the same Bus (as its input) as the one you use on that Send Slot where you activated the SendPan.

    ... now isn't that intuitive or what?

- ☑ At least, there is kind of a shortcut if you've paid attention to the previous page about the different ways on how to enable Sends on Faders. Select the **Sends on Faders** ❼ option from the Sends Menu of the same Send Slot that you want to access the Pan Send.
- ☑ But wait a minute, where is the Pan Control? Surprise, it is the Pan Control ❽ on the Channel Strip that is "repurposed" as the Send Pan when you are in Sends on Faders View ❺.
- ☑ Remember that in the previous examples I showed in the Sends on Faders section, the Channel Strips didn't have any Pan Controls? That's the reason why. The same way the Volume Faders (yellow) ❾ on a Channel Strip turn into Send Levels, the Pan Controls ❽ on a Channel Strip turn into the Send Pan. However, you will only see a Send Pan for that Send if it has been activated in the Send Menu by enabling the **Independent Pan** ❶ option ... make sense?

➡️ Sends Pan Workflow

Once you wrapped your head around that implementation of the Send Pan, let me show you an easier workflow:

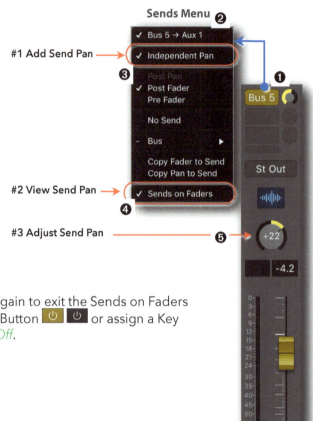

🟡 **Step 1: Add a Send Pan**

Click on the Send Slot ❶ where you want to add the Send Pan to open the Send Menu ❷ and enable the Independent Pan ❸ option. The ring turns yellow ❶.

🟡 **Step 2: Display a Send Pan**

Click on the Send Slot where you want to adjust the Pan Send to open the Send Menu and click on the Sends on Faders ❹ option.

🟡 **Step 3: Adjust a Send Pan**

Drag on the Pan Control ❺ of the Channel Strip that acts as the Send Pan, indicated by its yellow value ring.

🟡 **Stem 4: Exit Sends on Faders View**

Click on the Sends on Faders ❹ option in the Sends Menu again to exit the Sends on Faders View. It is easier to just click on Sends on Faders On/Off Button ⏻ ⏻ or assign a Key Equivalent to the Key Command *Sends on Faders - On/Off*.

➡️ Channel Width (Channel Format)

The Send Pan Control has the same features (power) as the Channel Pan Control. That means you can *right-click* on the Pan Control and select different types of controls depending on the Channel Width (Channel Format) of the Channel Strip.

▸ **Pan ❻**
▸ **Stereo Pan ❼**
▸ **Balance**
▸ **Surround Pan ❽**
▸ **Surround Balancer ❾** (this menu item is incorrect and should be labeled "Surround Panner").
▸ **Binaural Pan**

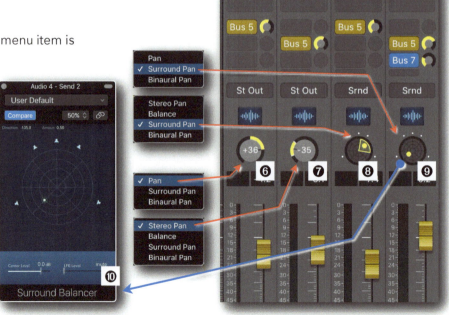

You can also *double-click* on the Surround Control to open the standalone window for the Surround Panner ❿ or Surround Balancer.

➡️ *Signal Flow Diagram*

Here is the signal flow diagram of a single Send Slot (please multiply that by 8 per Channel Strip) to illustrate its functionality we discussed so far.

🟡 *Send Pan*

The Send Pan ❶ component is only part of the signal flow in the Send Slot if it is enabled in the Send Menu, (**Independent Pan** selected ❷).

🟡 *Pre - Post*

The Sends Menu lets you select "where" ❸ you want to tap the signal along the Channel Strip that you send to a Bus. Logic gives you three options:

▶ **Pre Fader** ❹: The signal is tapped before the Channel Strip's Volume Fader, after the last Audio FX. This is common for headphone mixes or separate mixes that you want to be independent of the Volume Fader. Now with the additional Send Pan ❶, you have absolute freedom regarding the level and pan on that bus routing, which opens new possibilities.

▶ **Post Fader** ❺: The signal is tapped after the Volume Fader. This is common for FX sends.

▶ **Post Pan** ❻: This was the only option in previous Logic Pro X versions to have Pan control over the Send signal. However, it was always the same Pan Control from the Channel Strip and was after the Volume Fader, which is not what you want in some routing scenarios. Now that you have independent control over the Pan with the dedicated Send Pan ❶ in the Send Slot, this option is grayed out ❼ in the Send Menu when you have the Send Pan enabled ❷.

🟡 *Copy ... to Send*

The Sends Menu has two additional commands ❽:

▶ **Send Fader to Send** ❾: This is a useful command when you want to create a headphone mix using a Send. You select all Channel Strips that that should be part of your headphone mix, assign the Bus to a specific Send Slot and select this option. It will copy the current level of the Volume Fader of each Channel Strip to its Send so it is the same mix. After that, you can adjust the Sends independently.

▶ **Send Pan to Send**: ❿ This is the same concept, send the current level of the Channel Strip Pan to the Send Pan ❶ of that Send Slot, in case you had various pan positions in your mix.

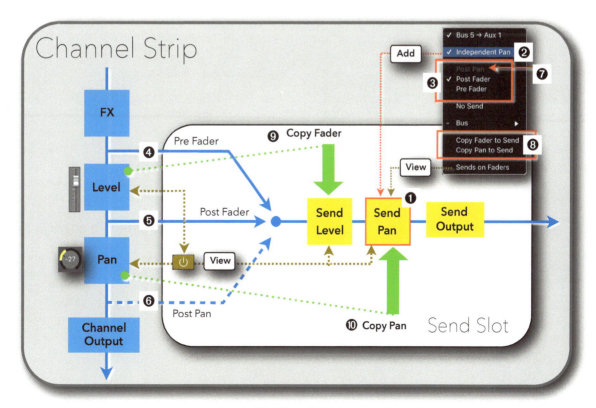

➡️ Color Code

Logic uses various colors to indicate a specific status. Make sure you can decipher all the possible color combinations and understand what they mean.

▶ **Blue** **Send Slot Button**: Default status when Sends on Faders View is disabled. That means the Volume Fader and Pan Control on the Channel Strip "belong" to the Channel Strip signal.

▶ **Yellow** **Send Slot Button**: Sends on Faders View is enabled. The Volume Fader on this Channel Strip (which is also yellow) controls the Send Level of this Send Slot. If the Pan Control is visible on the Channel Strip (yellow), then it is also the Pan Send of this Send Slot.

▶ **Blue** **Level Ring**: The Pan Control Knob is either Pre Fader (on the left) or Post Fader (positioned on the right).

▶ **Green** **Level Ring**: The Pan Control Knob is Post Pan

▶ **Yellow** **Level Ring**: The Send Slot has an independent Pan Control (**Independent Pan** option is selected in the Sends Menu). The Pan Control, however, is only visible if the Sends on Faders View is enabled (indicated by the yellow Send Slot Button). The Send is either Pre Fader (knob on the left) or Post Fader (knob on the right).

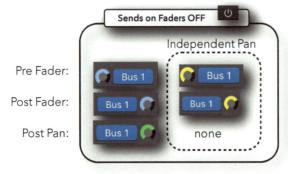
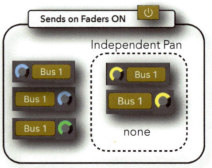

➡️ Great Opportunities

Once you digest all the new options and routing possibilities you will realize that there are great new routing scenarios you can use with those features:

🟡 Convenient Headphone Mixes

When you need to adjust the level of a headphone, you had to use those tiny rotary knobs on the Send Slots. Now you can switch to Sends on Faders View, choose the Return for the headphone mix and all the level controls are available as long (yellow) Faders to give you a nice overview and let you quickly and precisely adjust the balance of the headphone mix. Assigning a Key Command to the Sends on Fader On/Off ⏻ ⏻ command, to toggle the view with a single key.

🟡 Monitor Mixes for Stems

You can use Sends to create parallel Stem Mixes (Strings, Percussion, FXs) now with independent Pan control and convenient (yellow) Faders for level adjustments.

🟡 Create multiple Mixes

Because the Sends are after the Audio FX and now have independent Send Level and Send Pan, you can use a dedicated Send Slot as a separate mix bus with the corresponding Return function as its Output Channel Strip. Again, the Sends on Faders View lets you toggle between the two mixes to have their corresponding Faders and Pans available

🟡 Create Stereo and Surround Mixes in the same Project

You can easily create a Surround Mix in a Stereo Project or vice versa by using the Send Slots as the alternate Mix and choose the Pan Mode (Stereo Panner or Surround Panner) independently for each mix.

Smart Tempo

Smart Tempo was the big new feature that was introduced in Logic Pro X 10.4. It provides great new concepts and workflows on how to deal with Tempo and sets you free from the restraints of traditional tempo considerations in digital audio production.

There was a lot of confusion, misunderstanding, and misinformation on various YouTube videos that tried to "explain" Smart Tempo. Be careful because those videos are still out there and even commercial video series have inaccuracies about that topic. I can recommend Eli Krantzberg's video series at Groove3 who really understands Smart Tempo and demonstrates that feature very well. You can also read the more in-depth explanations on 30 pages in my previous book "Logic Pro X - What's New in 10.4"

➡ *Smart Tempo v2*

There are so many new features and improvements with Smart Tempo in Logic Pro X v10.4.2, almost like Smart Tempo v2.

Here are some of the highlights that I will explain in this chapter:
- Improved Smart Tempo Editor
- New and improved Smart Tempo Commands
- New Smart Tempo options in the Project Settings
- Smart Tempo for Multitrack
- Smart Tempo for MIDI with its own Smart Tempo Editor functionality

Smart Tempo Editor

There are many small and big changes in the Smart Tempo Editor, and yes, that is the first change, a name change. The "File Tempo Editor" is no called the "Smart Tempo Editor".

➡ *User Interface Changes*

⬤ *Smart Tempo Editor*

Although I would have preferred the term "Beat Marker Editor" (because that is what you are actually editing in that window), I think "Smart Tempo Editor" is a good choice too. At least, it is better than the term "File Tempo Editor", and now that Logic can use and edit the Smart Tempo also on MIDI Regions, that Editor Pane is also called Smart Editor.

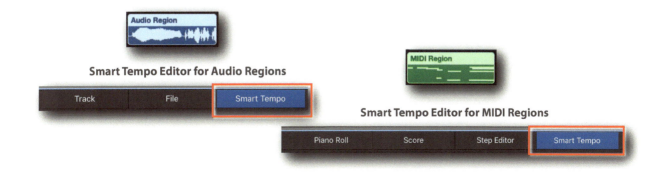

Smart Tempo Editor for Audio Regions

Smart Tempo Editor for MIDI Regions

● File Name

The File Name ❶ (the Parent Audio File of the currently selected Audio Region) is now displayed in a separate field ❷, which can turn into a popup menu with special functionality for multitrack files as we will see later.

● Actions Menu

Instead of the previous **Actions** ❸ menu, now you have two local menus, ❹ **Edit** and **View**. The previous commands have not only been moved to those new menus but also have slightly changed, and there are some important new commands.

● Catch Playhead

The Catch Playhead Button ❺ >Ⅰ< also has been moved to the left ❻.

● Tempo Curve Overlay

The Waveform Overview now can display the Tempo Track ❼ of that Audio File as an overlay based on the position of the Beat Markers.

● Downmix Overlay

The Main Waveform View can display the Downmix Waveform ❽ of multitrack files as a shaded overlay.

● Scroll Bars

The window now has a standard Scroll Bar ❾ at the bottom if you have zoomed into the Region and need to scroll left or right.

● Beat Marker Handles

The handle **Scale Left, Move Right** ❿ is now also available on Beat Markers, not only on Downbeat Markers.

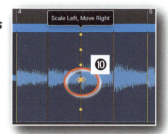

● Key Commands

The Key Commands (when the Smart Tempo Editor has key focus) have changed to be more consistent with other similar Key Commands in other windows.

- Key Command **Start or Stop Playback** has been replaced with Key Command **Preview** using the same Key Equivalent *opt+spacebar*.

- Key Command **Toggle Cycle** has been replaced with the Key Command **Cycle Audition On/Off** with the same Key Equivalent *ctr+C*

- Key Command **Toggle Catch** has been replaced with the Key Command **Catch Playhead Position** with the same Key Equivalent *`*.

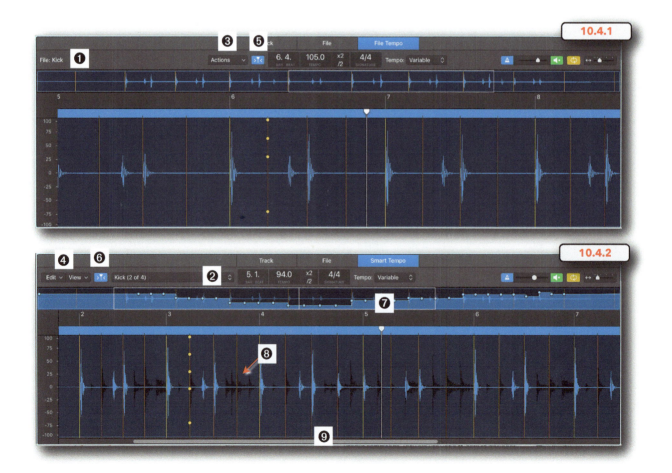

New Commands

One of the confusing parts of the Smart Tempo feature were the various commands. They were very long ❶, hard to decipher, and not consistent in the various locations they were listed in.

File Tempo Editor: Actions Menu

Adapt Project Tempo to Region Tempo and Align to Downbeat
Adapt Project Tempo and All Regions to Region Tempo and Downbeat
Adapt Region Tempo to Project Tempo and Align Downbeat

Maintain Time Position of All Regions   ❶

Revert Changes   `10.4.1`

Analyze Again
Revert to Original Recording Tempo
Remove Original Recording Tempo and Analyze Again

Set Average Tempo for Selection
Set Average Tempo within each Bar
Extend First Tempo in Selection to Beginning
Extend Last Tempo in Selection to End

Scroll in Play

➡️ *Locations*

Now, there are three locations where you can access the commands related to Smart Tempo. Those commands are now much more consistent, only with a few exceptions where commands are not applicable.

▶ **Main Menu**: The **Edit** menu has a menu item **Tempo** ❷ with a submenu containing all the Tempo commands. Those commands apply to the currently selected Region.

▶ **Local Menu**: As we have seen, the Smart Tempo Editor now has a Local Edit Menu ❸. It contains all the Smart Tempo commands.

▶ **Shortcut Menu**: *Right-click* on a Region ❹ to open its Shortcut Menu with the submenu **Tempo** ❺ that contains all the Smart Tempo commands.

Smart Tempo Editor

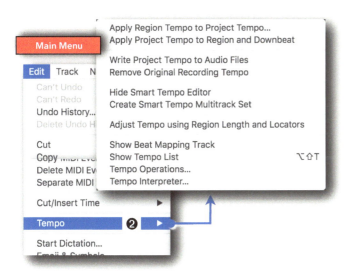

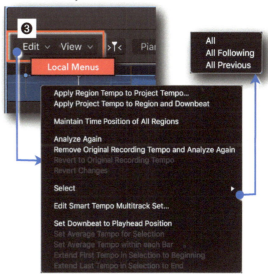

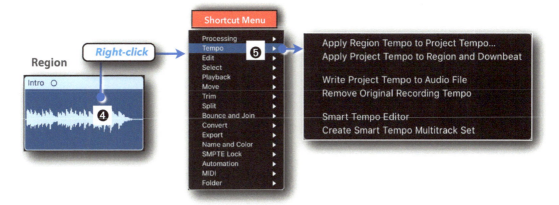

➡ **"Adapt" Changed to "Apply"**

One minor but very effective improvement with the commands is the change of one word. The wording "***Adapt*** *x to y*" has been changed to "***Apply*** *x to y*". This is a much better verb to indicate the "direction", which Tempo overwrite which Tempo.

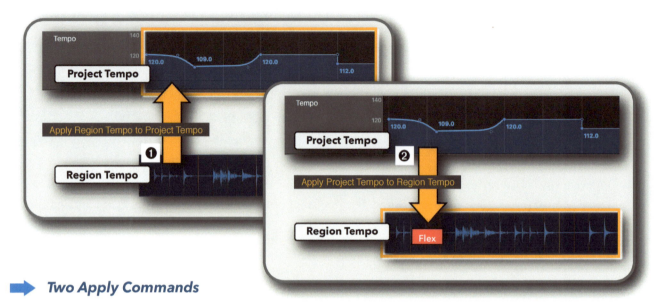

➡ **Two Apply Commands**

Another little improvement that makes those commands less confusing is to have only two "Apply" commands, one for each "direction" **Region ➤ Project ❶** and **Project ➤ Region ❷**. In 10.4.1 you had to carefully read ❸ before clicking on a command.

Now in all three menus (Main Menu, Local Menu, Shortcut Menu), those same two commands ❹ are always on top. The additional options for the **Apply Region Tempo to Project Tempo** command are now available in a separate dialog ❺ that opens when you choose that command (I especially like the "graphically enhanced" dialog, indicating the procedure with a little image ❻).

File Tempo Editor: Actions Menu

❸ Adapt Project Tempo to Region Tempo and Align to Downbeat
Adapt Project Tempo and All Regions to Region Tempo and Downbeat
Adapt Region Tempo to Project Tempo and Align Downbeat

10.4.1

☑ **Align downbeat to nearest project downbeat ❼**

If enabled, the procedure will have two steps. First, the selected Region will be shifted on the Track Lane so its first Downbeat Marker (the one that is marked in the Smart Tempo Editor) aligns to the closest downbeat in your Project (its Bars|Bets Grid). After that, the Region Tempo will be applied to the Project Tempo, which means the Project's Bars|Beats Grid will be aligned to the Downbeat Markers and Beat Markers of the Region (also applying the corresponding Time Signature).

☑ **Maintain relative position of all other regions ❽**

If the selected Region is shifted to align its downbeat, then it will be out of sync with the other Regions in your Workspace. This additional checkbox makes sure that those other Regions stay in sync and shift accordingly. Please note that when you change the Project Tempo (based on the selected Region Tempo) you have to make sure that all Audio Regions have Flex enabled or they play in the "wrong" tempo.

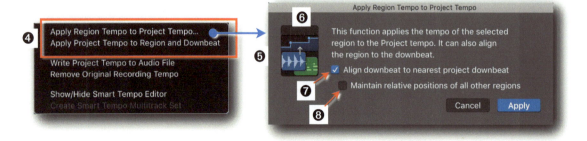

Smart Tempo - MIDI

Yes, Smart Tempo now works with MIDI recordings. The workflow and interface are similar or the same to Smart Tempo and audio recording.

➡️ Smart Tempo Editor

Although Smart Tempo uses the same Smart Tempo Editor for editing Audio Regions and MIDI Region, there is a little detail you have to be aware of.

🟡 Audio Region - File Tempo Editor

When you select an Audio Region ❶ in the Workspace and open the Editors Pane (Key Command *E*), you will see the three tabs ❷ for the three Audio Editors: **Track**, **File**, and **Smart Tempo**.

The Window Menu has a command **Open Smart Tempo Editor** ❸ (Key command *Open Smart Tempo Editor*). to open the Smart Tempo Editor as a standalone window (only if the Editor pane is not open at the same time).

🟡 MIDI Region - Region Tempo Editor

When you select a MIDI Region ❹ in the Workspace and open the Editors Pane ❺ (Key Command *E*), you will see four tabs for the four MIDI Editors: **Piano Roll**, **Score**, **Step Editor**, and **Smart Tempo**.

The Window Menu has a command **Open Smart Tempo Editor** ❸ (Key command *Open Smart Tempo Editor*). to open the Smart Tempo Editor as a standalone window (only if the Editor pane is not open at the same time).

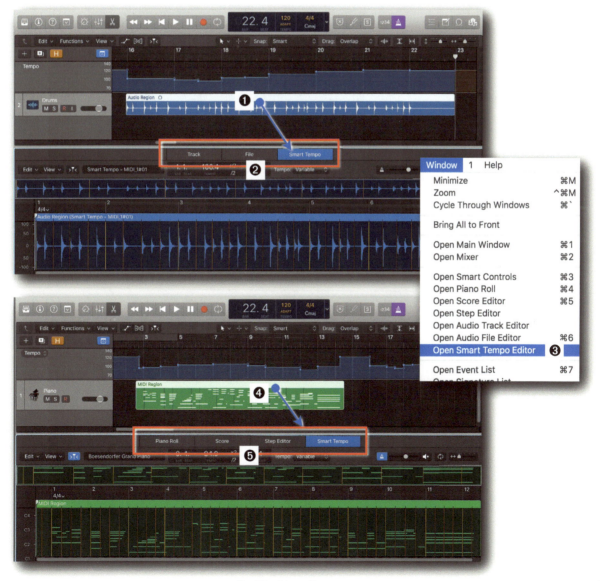

➡️ *ADAPT Tempo Mode*

Recording MIDI in ADAPT Tempo Mode works the same as recording audio, the same rules apply.

🟡 *Prepare*

Enable ADAPT Mode ❶ and make sure to turn off the Metronome, the Cycle Mode, and that there are no other Regions on any other Track in that time range you are about to record ❷.

🟡 *Record*

Press Record ❷ and play your MIDI Keyboard. Logic records the incoming MIDI Events, and you see the red Region ❸ expanding as you record.

🟡 *Smart Tempo*

Once you stop, Smart Tempo kicks into action:

- ☑ Logic shifts the new Region, so the first MIDI Event is aligned to a downbeat ❺ in your Project.
- ☑ Logic performs a tempo analysis of what you played to detect a tempo grid.
- ☑ That tempo grid is stored as Downbeat Markers and Beat Markers to the MIDI Region as the so-called Region Tempo.
- ☑ Logic automatically applies the command "**Apply Region Tempo to Project Tempo**" to create Tempo Events ❻ on the Project's Tempo Track based on the position of the Region's Beat Markers.

🟡 *Smart Tempo Editor*

Open the Smart Tempo Editor to make adjustments to the Beat Markers if necessary.

🟡 *MIDI Editing*

Remember, the MIDI Region plays back the same way you played it. Logic only figured out the tempo. It tells you in what Tempo you played your performance (including tempo changes) and aligns the Project's Tempo Track accordingly. Think about it, you can freely play a MIDI section and print it out as a score right away because your playing fits into the Project's Bars|Beats Grid.

- ☑ **Keep Tempo Track**: As long as you keep the Tempo Track, you keep the original tempo you performed, and now you can record additional tracks (MIDI and Audio) in that tempo.
- ☑ **Change Tempo Track**: You can change the Project's Tempo Track (maybe use a new Tempo Set so you can switch back to your original Tempo). Remember, the ADAPT Tempo Mode shifted the MIDI Region so it falls on the downbeat, so your MIDI recording is on the grid
- ☑ **Quantize MIDI**: Because your MIDI recording is on a Bars|Beats Grid, you can use the Quantize commands to quantize MIDI Events if necessary.
- ☑ **Edit MIDI**: Of course, you can Edit MIDI Events, as usual, using the other MIDI Editor.

KEEP Tempo Mode

While the ADAPT Tempo Mode automatically performs the tempo analysis and automatically adjusts the Project's Tempo Track, you can do all that later manually. For example, if you record a MIDI Region in standard KEEP Tempo Mode, open a Project with existing MIDI Regions, or import a MIDI Region that you don't know if it was recorded with or without a click.

Using Smart Tempo with MIDI Regions to quickly extract their tempo by using analysis based on machine learning algorithms instead of doing tedious, labor-intensive beat-mapping by hand is all new "territory" with new functionalities and concepts. However, to understand how it works and how to use it (without confusion and frustration) requires that you are familiar with the basic concepts of MIDI recording and how MIDI Regions function in Logic (and most other DAWs).

So let's start with those basics and see how Smart Tempo fits into all that.

⬤ *Project's Bars|Beats Grid*

The Ruler ❶ on top of the Workspace in Logic represents the Project's Bars|Beats Grid. This is also called the Musical Time or Relative Time because it doesn't indicate how long, for example, one bar or one beat last in Absolute Time of minutes and seconds. It is relative, depending on the Project Tempo.

⬤ *Project Tempo*

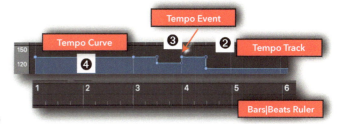

The Tempo Track ❷, one of the Global Tracks in Logic, determines the Tempo throughout the Project. A Tempo Event (that blue dot ❸) on the Tempo Track determines the Tempo Value (in bpm, "beats per minutes") from that Bars|Beats position until the next Tempo Event where the Project changes to the Tempo determined by that Tempo Event.

A Project with a consistent Tempo of 120bpm only has a single Tempo Event at the beginning of the Project and, therefore, the Tempo Curve ❹ on the Tempo Track is a flat line.

⬤ *MIDI Region*

When you record a MIDI signal, Logic creates a MIDI Region (always starts at the downbeat ❺ on or before the first recorded MIDI Event) and places the MIDI Events ❻ inside that MIDI Region ... but where?

Usually, when you start with a new Project, you use a Metronome that plays a click ❼ exactly at each Beat, so you have an audible orientation about that grid and when playing along, your musical phrase will be in reference to that grid. If you look at that MIDI Region in the Piano Roll Editor ❽, you will see the MIDI Events (the horizontal Note Bars) in reference ❾ to the vertical Bars|Beats Grid that is referenced to the Project's Bars|Beats Grid.

⬤ *Relative Note Reference*

The important thing to understand about the concept of MIDI Regions is that, although the notes you played each have an absolute length (based on the Project Tempo ❹ during the recording), the recorded MIDI Events ❻, on the other hand, don't have an absolute time value. The MIDI Events are just placed on the relative Bars|Beats Grid ❽. The Absolute Time of each recorded MIDI Event inside the MIDI Region (when and how long) is determined by the Project Tempo at that position.

For example, if you recorded the MIDI Events in 120bpm and then change the Tempo to 240bpm, then those same notes play back twice as fast and the duration of every single note is only half as long.

🟡 Region's Bars|Beats Grid

Think of each MIDI Region as kind of a mini-Project with its own Bars|Beats Grid, let's call it the Region's Bars|Beats Grid. The MIDI Events stored in that MIDI Region are placed along that grid. When you move a MIDI Region or import a MIDI Region that was recorded in a different Project (or different DAW), it has its own Bars|Beats Grid (Ruler) and by placing it somewhere on the Track Lane in your Project, the Region's Bars|Beats Grid aligns with the Project's Bars|Beats Grid and the MIDI Events inside the MIDI Region are played back based on the Project Tempo at that position.

Again, that MIDI Region has no absolute tempo information, only relative information. For example," *the first two notes are twice as long as the next two notes*" ❶ or "*there is more time between the first and the second note than between the third and the fourth*" ❷, etc.

This is a super important aspect that users are often not aware of about Standard MIDI Regions ❸. They don't carry any absolute tempo information. This will change because once Logic analyzes a MIDI Region, it will store absolute Tempo Information in this Region, I call it and Analyzed MIDI Region ❹.

> **Standard MIDI Regions**
> don't contain ❸
> Tempo Information

> **Analyzed MIDI Regions**
> do contain ❹
> Tempo Information

🟡 Smart Tempo Editor

Let's get our feet wet and select a Standard MIDI Region and see how it looks like in the Smart Tempo Editor ❺. Be careful, when the Smart Tempo feature was introduced for Audio Regions, many users assumed that the view in the Smart Tempo Editor was the same as the view in the Audio File Editor. The same misconception could happen here, so be aware, the Smart Tempo Editor displays a MIDI Region differently than the Piano Roll Editor ❻.

▶ The Main View shows the Note Bars ❼, which are read-only, you cannot edit them.

▶ The Ruler always starts at the beginning of the Region ❽, so be careful with the bar numbers. In this example, the MIDI Region starts at bar 2 (as you can see in the Piano Roll Editor), but in the Smart Tempo Editor, it starts at bar 1.

▶ The vertical orange lines are the Beat Markers, ❾ the Beat Markers on the downbeat are the Downbeat Markers ❿.

▶ If you enable the **Tempo Curve Overlay** option in the local View Menu, you can see the blue Tempo Curve ⓫ in the Overview Area. In this case, it is a constant tempo, 120bpm, a flat line.

▶ The other controls are pretty much the same as with the Smart Tempo for Audio Regions. One thing I want to point out is that the Preview Button 🔊 (Key Command *opt+spacebar*) only plays the Region "inside" this Smart Tempo Editor with its own Playhead moving along the Smart Tempo Editor's Ruler.

Please note that in this example we use the Smart Tempo Editor only to look at a Standard MIDI Region, a MIDI Region that hasn't been analyzed yet. It is just a different way to view the MIDI Region.

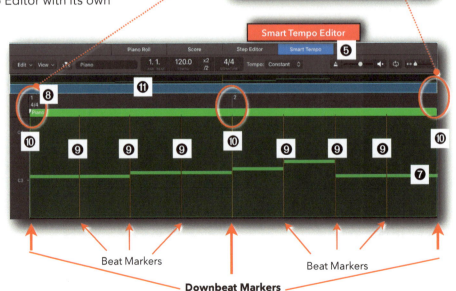

Beat Markers   Beat Markers

Downbeat Markers

● *Analyze*

Now when you select a Standard MIDI Region on a Track Lane and use the **Analyze** ❶ command (Smart Tempo Editor's local menu **Edit ➤ Analyze Again**), then Logic tries to detect the tempo of the performance recorded in that MIDI Region, for example, a piano part or a drum groove.

Apply Region Tempo to Project Tempo...
Apply Project Tempo to Region and Downbeat

Maintain Time Position of All Regions

Analyze Again ❶
Remove Original Recording Tempo and Analyze Again
Revert Changes

Set Average Tempo for Selection
Set Average Tempo within each Bar
Extend First Tempo in Selection to Beginning
Extend Last Tempo in Selection to End

There are many things that happen with this single command and I will demonstrate it with this simple musical phrase ❷ that I recorded without a click. As you can see on the screenshot of the Piano Roll Editor, the Note Bars ❸ don't align to the Region's Bars|Beats Grid.

Here are the seven steps that happen when I use the **Analyze** command on that MIDI Region:

▶ #1 - **Move Beat Markers**: Look at the Smart Tempo Editor in my example to understand that first action.

- The first screenshot ❹ shows the original MIDI Region ❸ with the Beat Markers ❺ presenting the Region's Bars|Beats Grid. As you can see, the MIDI Events are not on the grid, the same way they appear on the Piano Roll Editor ❸.

- The score ❻ illustrates what Logic detected in the Region, what it thinks the musical phrase could be. In this case, it analyzed correctly.

- The second screenshot ❼ of the Smart Tempo Editor shows that Logic is rearranging the Beat Markers ❽ to represent that musical phrase ❻ it detected.

- As you can see, the MIDI Events themselves are not moved (they haven't changed). Logic did only move the Beat Markers the way it thinks the phrase was played originally.

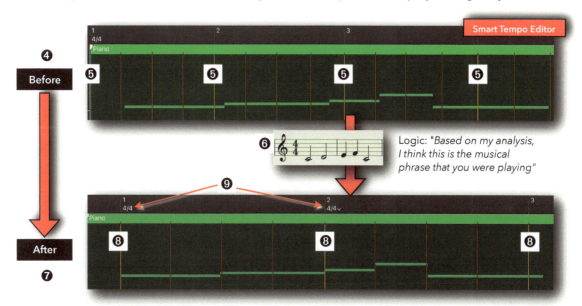

Logic: "*Based on my analysis, I think this is the musical phrase that you were playing*"

▶ #2 - **Region Bars|Beats Grid**: Those newly positioned Beat Markers now represent the (analyzed) Region's Bars|Beat Grid that will be stored with the Region and is different from the Project's Bars|Beats Grid because moving the Beat Markers created a different grid. However, the two grids are only temporarily different because the procedure is not completed yet. There are a few more steps.

▶ #3 - **Tempo Value**: The Region's Bars|Beats Grid has one specialty. Each Beat Marker has its own Tempo Value (that you can view in the Smart Tempo Editor) and each Downbeat Marker has the additional Time Signature Value ❾. Usually, when you record without a click, even if you play with a steady Tempo, you still will have slight tempo variations, and those will be picked up by the tempo analysis. Again, those Tempo Value and Time Signature Values for each Beat Marker and Downbeat Marker are stored with the MIDI Region, which is now a special Analyzed MIDI Region.

▶ #4 - **Align to Downbeat**: After Logic analyzed the MIDI Region and arranged the Beat Markers accordingly, it shifts ❶ the MIDI Region on the Track Lane so the first downbeat ❷ of the Region's Bars| Beats Grid (which is at the first MIDI Event in this example) aligns to the closest downbeat of the Project's Bars|Beats Grid.

▶ #5 - **Region Length Change**: This step is an important difference compared to analyzing Audio Regions. With MIDI Regions Logic automatically performs the command "**Apply Project Tempo to Region Tempo**". That means the Region's Bars|Beats Grid is aligned (moved) to the Project's Bars|Beats Grid and both grids are now the same ❸. The "shift" on the screenshot shows the effect in the Piano Roll Editor based on the (here invisible) Beat Markers defined in the Smart Tempo Editor.

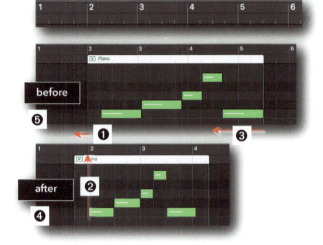

▶ #6 - **Region plays Project Tempo**: Because the original Region's Bars|Beats Grid has been adjusted, all the MIDI Events on that grid followed and moved accordingly (position and length of the Note Bar), which means the Region now plays at the Projects' Tempo. In this example, as you can see, the phrase is playing faster after ❹ the analysis than before ❺.

▶ #7 - **Stored Region Tempo Information**: This final step is the important housekeeping part that happens behind the scene. Aligning the Region's Bars|Beats Grid to the Project's Bars|Beats grid (in step #5) doesn't mean that the Region's Bars|Beats Grid will be overwritten. Logic has stored that information (as a result of the analysis procedure) with the MIDI Region (Position of the Beat Markers, Tempo Value of each Beat Marker, Time Signature of the Downbeat Markers). That's why I call this special MIDI Region "Analyzed MIDI Region". Remember, Standard MIDI Region, on the other hand, don't carry any Tempo Information!

⬤ *Change Tempo*

Once a MIDI Region has been analyzed and now fits the Project's Bars|Beats Grid. It behaves like any other Standard MIDI Region. It will follow any Tempo Changes in your Project. You can also move it around in your Workspace, and it will adapt to the current Tempo at the position you are moving it to.

⬤ *Retrieve Original Tempo*

The big difference between a Standard MIDI Region and an Analyzed MIDI Region is that the Analyzed MIDI Region contains Tempo Information, a Tempo Value (bpm) stored with each Beat Marker (and also Time Signature Information). That means when you use the command "**Apply Region Tempo to Project Tempo**" (*right-click* on a Region and choose from the Shortcut Menu), the following will happen:

Apply Region Tempo to Project Tempo

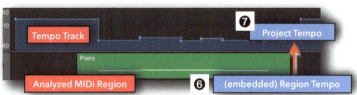

☑ The Project's Bars|Beats Grid is already aligned to the Region's Bars|Beats Grid, so nothing changes with the grid.

☑ Logic uses the Tempo Value stored in each Beat Marker of the Analyzed MIDI Region ❻ and creates a Tempo Event ❼ with that Tempo Value on the Project's Tempo Track. That has the effect that the MIDI Events now play back how they were performed (recorded) initially.

☑ An Analyzed MIDI Region also contains the Time Signature with each Downbeat Marker. If the Time Signature stored in the MIDI Region is different from the Time Signature on the Project's Time Signature Track, then Logic will create a new Time Signature with that value on the Project's Time Signature Track.

BTW: The other command "**Apply Project Tempo to Region Tempo**" is redundant because MIDI Regions (based on their nature) always follow any changes in the Project Track Lane. Remember, MIDI Events in MIDI Regions are stored as Relative Time referenced to the Bars|Beats Grid and not an absolute SMPTE timeline.

➡️ *Summary*

As you just saw, there is quite a lot of action going by using just one Analyze command. Here is a summary with the screenshots of the Piano Roll Editor and Smart Tempo Editor side-by-side. Try to keep that "mechanism" in mind when using the command to understand and predict what will happen. This is just a single MIDI Region, but when using that in a more "busy" Project with other Regions in the Workspace, you have to know what will happen and how it might affect other Regions (MIDI Regions and Audio Regions) in your Project.

▶ This is the musical phrase ❶ that I will play on my MIDI keyboard.

▶ I record the phrase with a click, and this is how the MIDI Events inside the recorded MIDI Region look like when viewed in the Piano Roll Editor ❷. The MIDI Events are aligned to the Bars|Beats Grid ❸.

▶ This is how the same MIDI Region looks like when viewed in the Smart Tempo Editor ❹. Only the bar numbering is different, using the relative numbering of the Region.

▶ Now I record the same phrase little bit slower and without a click in the same Project. Now, this is how the MIDI Events inside the recorded MIDI Region look like when viewed in the Piano Roll Editor ❺. The MIDI Events are not aligned to the Bars|Beats Grid because they represent a different Tempo.

▶ This is how this MIDI Region looks like when viewed in the Smart Tempo Editor ❻. The Beat Markers still represent the original Region's Bars|Beats Grid and like in the Piano Roll Editor don't align to the grid.

▶ Now I apply the **Analyze** ❼ command in the Smart Tempo Editor, and as you can see, the Beat Markers are moved ❽ to align with the musical phrase.

▶ On the Piano Roll Editor ❾, you can see what the **Analyze** command also did. It shifted the Region so the first MIDI Event (which now has a Downbeat Marker aligned to it) is aligned to the closes downbeat of the Project's Bars|Beats Grid and the entire Region has been stretches or squeezed (here it is squeezed) so the new Region's Bars|Beat Grid (based on the repositioned Beat Markers) aligns to the Project's Bars|Beats Grid ❸.

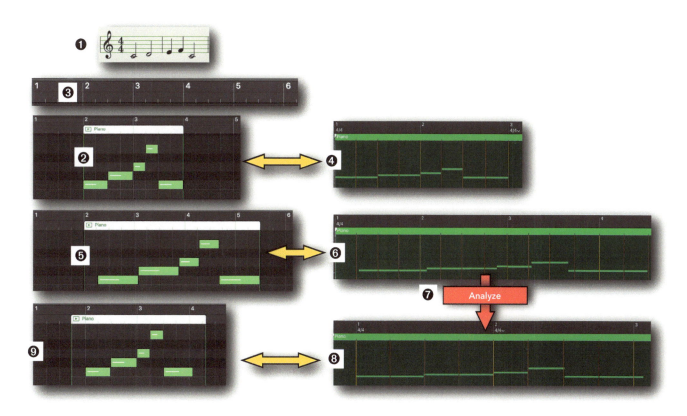

Of course, this is a very simplified example, but hopefully it helps to demonstrates the concept and the underlying processes that happen when using the Smart Tempo feature on MIDI Regions.

Smart Tempo Editor

The tempo analysis may not always provide perfect results, depending on the complexity of the musical phrases and the algorithm of the analysis program. That means you might have to make some manual adjustments in the Smart Tempo Editor.

● **Editing**

You can perform three main tasks in the Smart Tempo Editor (I explain them in more details in my book "Logic Pro X - What's New in 10.4":

- ☑ Adjust the position of the Beat Markers and Downbeats Markers using the various handles ❶.
- ☑ Define the Downbeat Markers. Especially with musical phrases that start with pickup notes, Logic might falsely pick the first MIDI Event as the downbeat.
- ☑ Change the Time Signature ❷ on Downbeat Markers as needed.

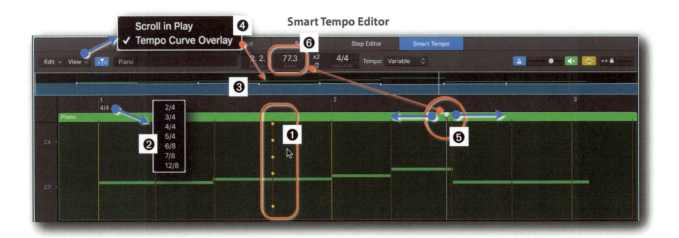

● **Tempo Information**

When you have already analyzed a MIDI Region and open the Smart Tempo Editor, you can see its embedded Tempo Information as a blue Tempo Curve ❸ in the Overview Area when you selected **Tempo Curve Overlay ❹** in the local View Menu.

You can also *drag* ❺ along the Ruler Area (the local Playhead will follow), and the Tempo value of the Beat Markers at that position is shown in the Tempo Display ❻.

● **Other Controls**

The other controls in the Smart Tempo Editor work the same as when using them with Audio Regions.

● **Trim to Region start**

This is a general tip when using Smart Tempo in your Project. Always trim MIDI Regions to the downbeat. There is a lot of analyzing, calculating, and shifting going on under the hood, and it seems that Logic can get confused if a MIDI Region doesn't start on a downbeat.

Remember, Logic has these mysteries with "unstable conditions", for example, when the first bar of a Project starts before bar 1 ❼.

Multitrack Recording

Initially, when the Smart Tempo feature was introduced in Logic Pro X 10.4, it was restricted to single Audio Files (Audio Regions). The Logic update v10.4.1 then also allowed to use multitrack recording with Smart Tempo. Now with this Logic Pro X version 10.4.2, multitrack recording has been further improved with many additional tools for using Smart Tempo with multitrack recording, for example, recording a multitrack session freely in ADAPT Mode.

There are lots of new features and workflow steps (some of them a little bit hidden) that you have to make yourself familiar with. I will introduce them step by step.

➡️ **Overview**

Let's start with an overview to better understand the concept and essential components that we will encounter in the various user interface elements.

⬤ **Single Audio Region**

When using Smart Tempo on a single Audio Region ❶, then you have only one component.

> **Tempo Analysis**
>
> Each Audio File is tempo-analyzed ❷ individually. The tempo grid (made up of Downbeat Markers and Beat Markers) that is detected is saved as Tempo Information ❸ to the audio file ❹ as metadata. Any time you are editing the Downbeat Markers and Beat Markers in the Smart Tempo Editor, the updated Tempo Information is saved to the file ❹.

⬤ **Multiple Audio Regions**

There are common scenarios (multitrack recording and Stems) where you have to treat multiple audio files ❺ as a group, and those audio files have to stay in sync when you edit them, and that also includes Smart Tempo. For example, using Tempo Analysis only on one file of that group would shift it if you use any Smart Tempo operations and the group of files would be out of sync.

Logic uses two main components when applying Smart Tempo to a group of audio files.

> **Grouped Tempo Analysis**
>
> Logic analyzes ❻ all audio files in that group to come up with a single tempo grid that represents the tempo that is performed in those audio files. That same Tempo Information ❼ is stored to each audio file ❽ as metadata. Editing any Region in the Smart Tempo Editor will update the Tempo Information and will be saved to all audio files in that group.

> **Smart Tempo Multitrack Set**

Logic organized all the files in that group in a so-called Smart Tempo Multitrack Set ❾, similar to an Audio File Group in the Project Audio Browser. A separate window gives you control over that set to allow some configuration. Also, the Smart Tempo Multitrack Set also produces a new audio file ❿, a downmix of all the audio files in that set which provides some useful editing tools in the Smart Tempo Editor.

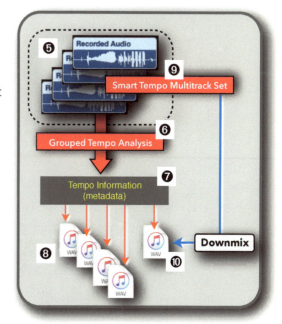

Grouped Tempo Analysis

So one of the main components of the Smart Tempo feature that enables the functionality with multitrack recordings is the Grouped Tempo Analysis. Logic has to make sure that all the audio files that belong to a group of audio files that originate from a multitrack recording or belong to a group of Stems (which are submixes of a Project, for example, "All Strings", "All Percussions", "All Vocals", a practice often used when delivering a film scoring project) are treated as a group. That means if the Tempo Information of one file is changed, Logic automatically has to change the Tempo Information of all the other files in that group accordingly, so they stay in sync.

To do that, Logic is using an existing feature, the Audio File Group, and slightly modifies its functionality.

⚫ *Audio File Group - manually*

This is the basic functionality of the Audio File Group:

▶ **Flat List**: Every new Audio File that you record in your Project or import to your Project is listed in the Project Audio Browser ❶ in one "flat" list ❷, and depending on your Project, that list could get pretty long.

▶ **Audio Files and Audio Regions**: The list shows all the Audio Files ❸ (that function as folders on that list), and by *clicking* on their disclosure triangle on the left of that row, you can "open" that folder to reveal all the Audio Regions ❹ that are based on that Parent Audio File. *Opt+click* on a disclosure triangle expand/collapse all files.

▶ **Create Group**: Logic provides a feature that lets you create folders in that list, so-called Audio File Groups ❺, and lets you move Audio Files ❻ into those folders to better organize your Audio Files and, of course, their Audio Regions that are listed underneath each Parent Audio File. There are many different procedures how to create or delete those folders ❼ and move files in and out of those folders. If you want to brush up on that topic, I recommend my book "Logic Pro X - The Details".

▶ **Name Field**: You can name the folder by *double-clicking* on the **Name** field of that row. In this example, I created a group for the four Audio Files ❻ of the drum recording and, therefore, name the group "**Drums**" ❽. Pay attention to that field later when using Smart Tempo.

▶ **Info Field**: The info field of the folder has the name "**Audio file group**" ❾ to indicate that this row represents a folder. You can rename that field. Also, pay attention to this field when using Smart Tempo.

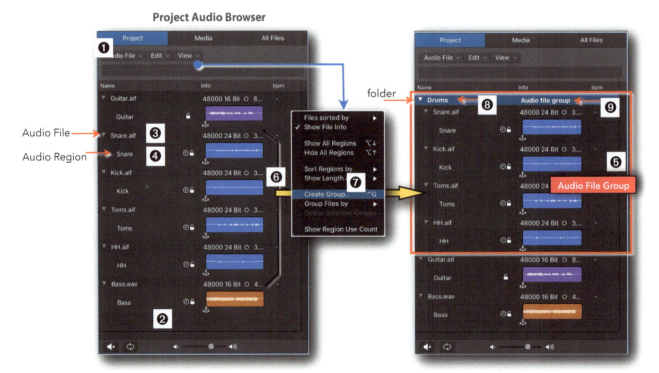

Project Audio Browser

🟡 *Audio File Group - automatically*

Logic Pro X 10.4.2 extends the functionality of the Audio File Group in regards to Smart Tempo and multitrack recording. Here is a demonstration:

▶ **Step 1: Record individual Tracks:** In this Project, I recorded a short phrase on the Guitar Track ❶ and, after that, a phrase on the Bass Track ❷. Their Audio Regions are listed in the Project Audio Browser as two entries ❸.

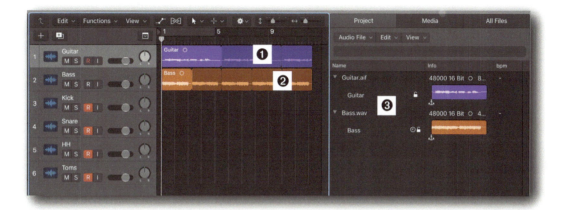

▶ **Step 2: MultiTrack Recording**: Now I do a multitrack recording, recording the four tracks (Kick, Snare, HH, Toms) at the same time ❹.

▶ **Step 3: Result**: If you look at the Project Audio Browser now, you can see the new functionality.

☑ Logic created a folder with the name "**Multitrack Set 1**" ❺

☑ All the four Audio Files of that multitrack recording that I just did are automatically placed in that folder.

☑ The **Info** field is empty ❻, it does not have the name "**Audio file group**" like when I create a folder manually, but you can name it if you want to by *double-clicking* on the field.

● *Audio File Group - New Functionality*

What you see next is one of the new functionality in Logic regarding multitrack recording.

▸ When you record multiple Tracks ❶ in KEEP Mode, then Logic automatically creates an Audio File Group ❷ in the Project Audio Browser.

▸ This Audio File Group has two new functionalities:

☑ Grouped Tempo Analysis: When you select one Audio Region ❸ of that group and open the Smart Tempo Editor ❹, then any edits you make for that Audio File (Tempo Information) will also be applied to any other file of that group ❶ ❷.

☑ Name popup menu: When you select one Audio Regions ❸ of that group and open the Smart Tempo Editor ❹, then the File Name field ❺ is now a popup menu that lists all the Audio Regions ❻ of that group. This way you can quickly switch between files from within the Smart Tempo Editor.

▸ This new functionality now applies to all Audio File Groups, the ones created automatically (with multitrack recording in KEEP Mode) and the ones you create manually.

▸ Be careful; despite the name **Multitrack Set**, this is not a Smart Tempo Multitrack Set, one of the main components I introduced earlier. I will demonstrate that in a moment.

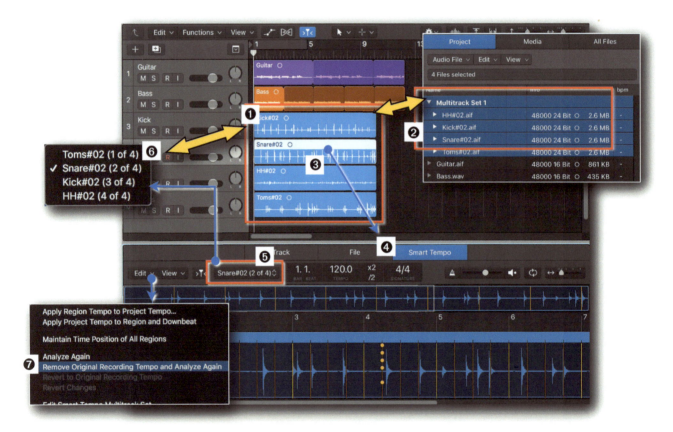

Be Aware!

Please note that I recorded this example in Keep Tempo Mode. That means that all the Audio Files will inherit the Tempo Information of the Project's Tempo Track at that corresponding timeline position. Any of those Tempo Events will be saved to those Audio Files as metadata. This Tempo Information is called the "Original Recording Tempo". That means these files don't contain any Analyzed Tempo information because they haven't been tempo-analyzed yet by Smart Tempo. On the other hand, when you record in ADAPT Tempo Mode, then Smart Tempo will perform the Tempo Analysis during the recording and stores the tempo-analyzed data as Tempo Information in each individual files.

When you open an Audio Region in the Smart Tempo Editor that only contains the Original Recording Tempo, you have to use the command "**Remove Original Recording Tempo and Analyze Again**" ❼.

Smart Tempo Multitrack Set

Now let's look at the second main components of the Smart Tempo functionality for multitrack recording, the Smart Tempo Multitrack Set. It is a slightly complex component, but you have to wrap your head around it to understand the Smart Tempo feature and properly use it.

⬤ Create it Manually

Continuing with the previous example, I want to demonstrate the basic functionality of a Smart Tempo Multitrack Set.

- ▶ **Group Members**: First, you have to select all the Audio Regions ❶ in the Workspace that belongs to the multitrack recording or the Stems that you want to group into a Smart Tempo Multitrack Set.
- ▶ **Why**: Remember, in our example, all those Regions are already part of an Auto File Group, so they are analyzed and treated together. The reason for this step is to add more functionality as we will see in a moment.
- ▶ **Create**: *Right-click* on one of the selected Regions ❷ and choose from the *Shortcut Menu ➤ Tempo* submenu the command "**Create Smart Tempo Multitrack Set**" ❸.
- ▶ **Dialog**: The Smart Tempo Multitrack Set Dialog ❹ opens that lists all the Regions ❺ that I had selected ❶ in the Workspace. I explain the details in a moment. For now, click the **Update** ❻ button.

Look at the Project Audio Browser ❼ to see what has happened.

- ☑ A new folder (a new row ❽) has been created. That is the new Smart Tempo Multitrack Set.
- ☑ So a Smart Tempo Multitrack Set is just a special Audio File Group.
- ☑ Its **Name** field lists "**Smart Tempo MultiTrack Set 2**" ❾.
- ☑ Its **Info** field lists "**for Smart Tempo**" ❿. This field cannot be renamed. It is the indication that this Audio File Group is a Smart Tempo Multitrack Set.
- ☑ The previous Audio File Group **Multitrack Set 1** ⓫ now is empty because all its files have been moved to this special Audio File Group.

● Downmix File

So by creating a Smart Tempo Multitrack Set, nothing has changed regarding the Grouped Tempo Analysis. All the Regions are still part of a (special) Audio File Group, and their Tempo Information will still be edited together.

However, one specialty about the Smart Tempo Multitrack Set happened behind the scene.

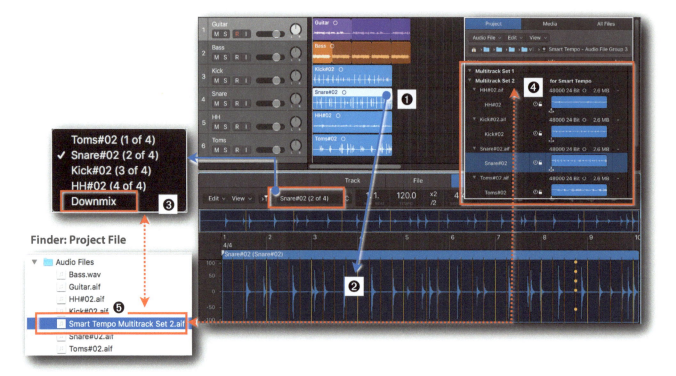

- ▶ **Downmix Option**: When you select any of the Audio Regions ❶ in that group in the Workspace to view it in the Smart Tempo Editor ❷ you will notice a difference in the Audio File name popup menu. In addition to the Audio Files in that group that are listed in that popup menu, it has a new option at the bottom of the list, named **Downmix** ❸.

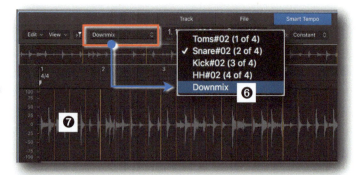

- ▶ **Downmix File**: What happened when you created the Smart Tempo Multitrack Set ❹, is that Logic bounced all the Audio Files in that group to a new Audio File. If you peek inside the Project File (the **Audio Files** folder inside the **Media** folder), you can see a new audio file ❺ named after this Audio File Group.

- ▶ **Downmix View**: When selecting the Downmix ❻ option from the popup menu, the Smart Tempo Editor will display the waveform ❼ of that down-mixed audio file (gray, without Region color). This could help in editing the Beat Markers because you can see all the audio signals.

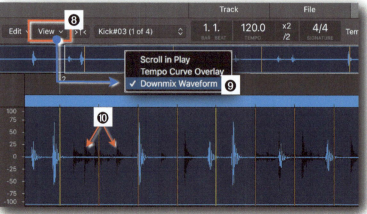

- ▶ **Downmix Waveform Overlay**: Now the local View Menu ❽ also lists a new option **Downmix Waveform** ❾ that, when enabled, displays the waveform of the down-mixed audio file as a darker overlay on the main waveform view.

Different Scenarios

Keep in mind that there are many different variations on how to work with multitrack recordings in regards to Smart Tempo. It is very easy to get lost because each different workflow may result in a different appearance of the components, variations of available commands and different outcome of various procedures.

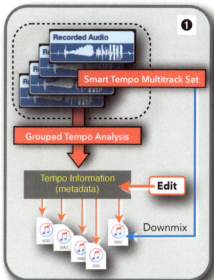

Here are a few scenarios regarding newly created or existing multitrack recordings. Always keep the underlying concept ❶ in mind.

Record in ADAPT Mode

☑ **Multitrack Set**: The Smart Tempo Multitrack Set is automatically created containing all the Audio Regions that are recorded during a take.

☑ **Analyze**: All the recorded Audio Files are tempo-analyzed as a group during the recording, and the Tempo Information is stored in each file after you stop the recording.

Record in KEEP Mode

☑ **Multitrack Set**: Only an Audio File Group is created containing all the Audio Regions that are recorded during that take. Select all Audio Regions after the recording and create a Smart Tempo Multitrack Set manually.

☑ **Analyze**: Audio Files are not analyzed. Only the Project's Tempo Track is stored as Tempo Information to all Audio Files in that group. Select one of the files and use the command "**Remove Original Recording Tempo and Analyze Again**". That new (analyzed) Tempo Information is automatically stored to each Audio File in that group as the new Tempo Information and replaces the old one.

Open existing Project

☑ **Multitrack Set**: Select all the Audio Regions that belong to the multitrack group or the stems and manually create a Smart Tempo Multitrack Set.

☑ **Analyze**: Open the Smart Tempo Editor and use the command "**Remove Original Recording Tempo and Analyze Again**" to remove any existing tempo Information on all files and group-analyze the files to retrieve their tempo. That new tempo is automatically stored to each Audio File in that group as the new Tempo Information.

Import Files

☑ **Multitrack Set**: When dragging files from the Finder or the All Files Browser (which is kind of a Finder built into Logic) directly onto the Workspace, then the Add Selected Files to Tracks Dialog ❷ pops up with a new checkbox "**All selected files are stems from one project**" ❸. The status of this checkbox determines the following:

Add Selected Files to Tracks Dialog

☑ **Checked**: Logic will automatically create a new Smart Tempo Multitrack Set for those imported files.

◾ **Unchecked**: Logic will import the files as individual files without creating any Audio File Group in the Project Audio Browser.

☑ **Analyze**: The question about whether the files are analyzed or not depends on the imported files (do they already contain Tempo Information?) and the configuration in the Smart Tempo Project Settings.

Edit Group (Group Inspector)

There is one important aspect when working with multitrack files, even before Smart Tempo came along, and that is a so-called **Edit Group**.

Main Inspector

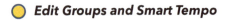

⬤ Edit Groups

- ▶ **Channel Strip Groups**: Logic's Group ❶ feature, also called Chanel Strip Groups, lets you group Channel Strips so when adjusting a control on one Channel Strip, for example, the Volume Fader, moves the Fader accordingly on all other Channel Strips that belong to that same Group.

- ▶ **Settings**: Each Group has a **Settings** ❷ section where you can select which control is linked between those grouped Channel Strips.

- ▶ **Editing (Selection) Options**: One of those settings is **Editing (Selection)** ❸, which links most of the editing tasks in the Workspace for the Tracks of the corresponding Channel Strips.

- ▶ **Edit Groups**: The **Editing** option is recommended for Tracks that are recorded as multitrack to make sure that any edit affects all Regions of the multitrack recording. This is also referred to as an "Edit Group".

- ▶ **Quantize Locked**: If **Editing** is enabled, another option becomes available **Quantize-Locked (Audio)** ❹ that guarantees that all the Regions are phase-locked when they are moved to avoid any phase shifting between the tracks that could negatively impact the sound of the recording due to phase cancelations. The Track Header on all those Tracks now displays the green Q Button ❺ Q .

⬤ Edit Groups and Smart Tempo

Although the tempo analysis is performed for the entire group of multitrack recorded Audio Files, it is highly recommended to create a Channel Strip Group for all the Tracks of that multitrack recording and enable Edit Group for it. This guarantees that any edits, in the Smart Tempo Editor or the Region itself in the Workspace are always phase-locked when Regions got shifted.

The Smart Tempo Project Setting ❻ has a new checkbox "**Create matching Edit group when creating Smart Tempo Multitrack Set**" ❼. And that is exactly what happens in any of the following scenarios:

- ☑ When you do a multitrack recording in ADAPT Mode, Logic automatically creates a Channel Strip Group for those Tracks with **Editing Selection** ❸and **Quantize-Lock** ❹ enabled.

- ☑ When you do a multitrack recording in KEEP Mode, Logic automatically creates a Channel Strip Group for those Tracks with the Editing Selection and Quantize-Lock enabled.

- ☑ You manually create a Smart Tempo Multitrack Set.

- ☑ When you import a group of multitrack file or stems with the checkbox "**All selected files are stems from one project**" ❽ enabled.

Smart Tempo Project Settings

Smart Tempo Multitrack Set Dialog

Now let's have a closer look at the window that enables you to configure a Smart Tempo Multitrack Set, the Smart Tempo Multitrack Set Dialog.

⬤ Open the Dialog

The command to open the dialog is available in three locations:

- Main Menu *Edit ➤ Tempo ➤*
- Smart Tempo Editor local *Edit Menu ➤*
- *Right-Click* on a Region and select from the *Shortcut Menu ➤ Tempo ➤*

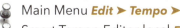

The command is slightly different depending on the following circumstances:

- **Create Smart Tempo Multitrack Set** (grayed out) ❶ if you have only selected one Region, or the Regions are not applicable.
- **Create Smart Tempo Multitrack Set** ❷ if you have selected more than one Region. *Clicking* on the command opens the Smart Tempo Multitrack Set Dialog to create a new set.
- **Edit Smart Tempo Multitrack Set** ❸ if the selected a Region is already part of a Smart Tempo Multitrack Set. *Clicking* on the command opens the Smart Tempo Multitrack Set Dialog to edit the set.

⬤ Analyze or Update

Please note that the dialog shows either an **Analyze** button or an **Update** button.

▸ **Analyze** ❹: This indicates that the files in that set don't contain any Tempo Information. *Click* on the button to create the set and perform a tempo analysis on those files

▸ **Update** ❺: This indicates that the files already contain Tempo Information. *Click* on the button to update the set with any changes made in that window.

⬤ Add/Remove Regions to/from the Set

The dialog doesn't allow you to add or remove Regions to/from the set. The only way to do that is in the Project Audio Browser by *dragging* an Audio File into an Audio File Group or *drag* it out of the Audio File Group to put back on the top level of the Project Audio Browser.

🟡 **Edit/Manage _Smart Tempo Multitrack Set_**

These are the elements in the dialog window:

▶ **Regions/Files in the Set**

The first two columns ❶ of the dialog list the name of the Audio Regions (**Regions**) and their Parent Audio File (**Used File**) in that set. These are read-only files.

If the set contains multiple Regions that belong to the same Parent Audio File, then the list will have only one row for that Audio File and all its Regions are listed in the first column, separated by a comma.

Smart Tempo Multitrack Set Dialog

▶ **Contribute to Analysis**

By enabling a checkbox ❷, you can determine which of the Region is used when Logic performs the combined tempo analysis. For example, if you have a multitrack recording of a drum set with ten microphones, then you can choose only the kick and snare mic to be used for the analysis or only the overhead mics. Or if you have a recording of a complete band, you can choose only the drums.

Remember, based on the analysis data, Logic determines one Tempo Track that is saved to each of the files of that set, regardless whether those files were part of the analysis or not.

Warning: Only the files with an enabled checkbox ☑ will be included in the Downmix file! Changing the checkboxes and clicking **Update**, will create a new Downmix file. That, of course, will also affect the various views in the Smart Tempo Editor (local menu _View ➤ **Downmix Waveform**_).

▶ **Regions need to be Bounced**

Logic requires that all the Regions in that set have the same start time. It uses the Region(s) with the earliest start time as a reference, and if any Region starts later, it will be indicated in that fourth column, telling you how many Regions Logic need to bounce, a procedure necessary to perform the proper tempo analysis

If you _click_ the **Update** button in such a case, the following will happen:

☑ Logic bounces that ("too late") Region to a new file with the added space at the beginning, so it starts at the same time as the other Regions in that set.

☑ That newly bounced Audio File (with the word "**merged**" added to the file name) will be added to the set, and the original Audio File will be removed from the set.

☑ You can then see in the Project Audio Browser, that the new "merged" file is now inside the Smart Tempo Multitrack Set folder and the original file is moved outside that folder, not belonging to the set anymore.

☑ Logic automatically replaced the original Region with a trimmed version of the new "merged" Audio File, so it has the same length on the Workspace as the original (pre-bounced) Region.

▶ **Break Up Set**

The **Break Up Set** button removes the Smart Tempo Multitrack Set:

☑ On the Workspace, the Audio Regions still look the same

☑ The Audio File Group in the Project Audio Browser, the folder that contained all the Regions belonging to that set, will be removed and all the Files are now listed on the top level as any other Audio File in the Project Audio Browser.

☑ Each Audio File still keeps the embedded Tempo Information that was created when it was a member of that set. Remember, the result of the tempo-analysis, the Region Tempo, was saved to each Audio File that was a member of that set.

Other Smart Tempo Additions and Changes

➡ *Automatic Enable Flex on "Apply Project Tempo to Region and Download"*

Remember that there are two "directions" when dealing with "applying" Tempo. Either you apply the Region Tempo to the Project Tempo or the other way around, apply the Project Tempo to the Region Tempo. The second one where you use the Tempo Information in the Tempo Track of the Project (fixed tempo or with tempo changes) and force that onto the Region, so it follows (adapts to) the Project Tempo only works when two conditions are met:

☑ **Analyzed Audio**: The Audio Region has to be tempo-analyzed so it contains Beat Markers that represents the tempo grid of that Audio Region, which can be moved accordingly.

☑ **Flex Enabled**: Flex has to be enabled for the Region, so Logic can move the Beat Markers of the Audio Region to the Tempo Markers of the Project, and because the Beat Markers act as Flex Markers, they flex the audio accordingly based on the shifting of the Beat Markers.

Previous Logic versions required that you knew that second requirements and manually enabled Flex. Now, when you use the command "**Apply Project Tempo to Region and Downbeat**" ❶, Logic automatically enables Flex and Follow (on ❷) and also enables Flex ❸ on that Track, with the **Polyphonic** algorithm selected.

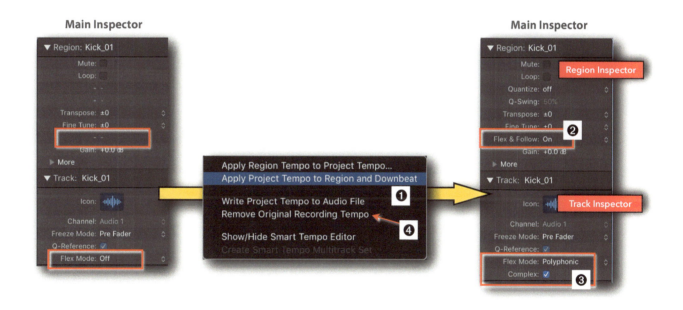

➡ *Batch Delete File Tempo Information Dialog*

When you use the command **Remove Original Recording Tempo**, you get a Warning Dialog ❺ that you cannot undo this action. Prior to 10.4.2 , if you had multiple Regions selected to apply that command to all those Regions, you had to click away that Dialog for each Region. Now, that dialog applies to all Regions and you have to click the **OK** button only once.

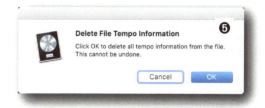

➡️ Export Tempo Resolution

The Smart Tempo Project Settings ❶ has a new parameter **Export Tempo Resolution** ❷ with two options ❸. Be aware that, despite the text explanation, this setting will also affect any recording in ADAPT mode or when using the **Apply Region Tempo to Project Tempo**.

▶ **Beats**: All tempo actions, will create the Tempo Information in beat resolution, one Tempo Value per Beat Marker. That means that any result in the Smart Tempo Editor will be exactly exported as is.

▶ **Smoothed**: The smoothed resolution is more suitable when you Flex the Regions to Beats. However, as soon as nothing should be flexed, the Beats Resolution delivers a way more accurate result and is often the better choice.

Project Settings ➤ Smart Tempo

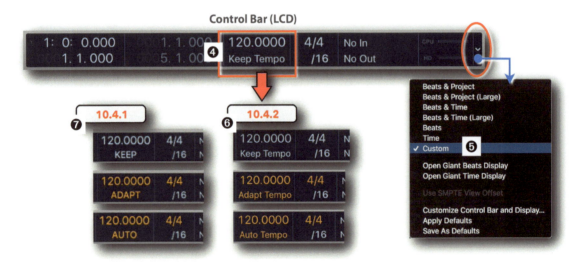

➡️ Custom Display Mode

The Tempo Display ❹ in the Control Bar LCD has changed slightly when the Custom Display Mode ❺ is selected. Now ❻, it displays **Keep Tempo**, **Adapt Tempo**, or **Auto Tempo** instead of just **KEEP**, **ADAPT**, or **AUTO** ❼.

Control Bar (LCD)

➡️ Manually Create Ritardando/Accelerando

If the automatic tempo detection doesn't catch a ritardando (gradual tempo decrease) or accelerando (gradual tempo increase), then you have to edit the Beat Markers manually in the Smart Tempo Editor using the **Scale Left, Move Right** handle.

☑ **10.4.1**: In 10.4.1, Logic inserted additional bars when moving the Beat Markers to far, making it impossible to properly place the Beat Markers to reflect a sudden ritardando or accelerando.

☑ **10.4.2**: Now in 10.4.2, you can create those tempo changes without a problem.

Set Downbeat to Playhead Position

The Local Edit Menu in the Smart Tempo Editor has a new command "**Set Downbeat to Playhead Position**". Of course, this refers to the Playhead in the Smart Editor and not in the Workspace.

You place the Playhead at a position along the Ruler in the Smart Tempo Editor and when using this command, the entire grid of Beat Markers will move accordingly like when using the "**Move All**" Handle.

 ### *Snap to Transients*

This is not a new feature, but because many users are not aware of it, I want to mention it here.

Whenever you use any of the Handles on a Beat Marker to move them along the waveform, you can hold down the *command* key and all the Beat Markers will snap to the closest transient.

The important little detail to pay attention to is that each Beat Marker acts independently to determine when it is close enough to a transient to snap to it. Just try it and you will see the effect.

 ### *Flex and Movie Files*

There are few changes with Flex when using Movie Files:

- ☑ Logic Pro now displays a warning when opening a SMPTE-locked audio file extracted from a movie when the audio file is opened in the Smart Tempo Editor.
- ☑ Movie position now changes position as expected when "**Apply Region Tempo to Project Tempo**" is used with the checkbox "**Maintain relative positions of all other regions**" enabled
- ☑ The start position of a movie now adjusts correctly when the "**Adapt Project Tempo and all Regions top project Tempo and Downbeat**" command is used.

 ### *A Few Tips*

When editing a Smart Tempo Multitrack Set in the Smart Tempo Editor, you can try the following to find the best analysis result with difficult audio material:

- ☑ In the Smart Tempo Editor, select one of the Regions in that group that might get you the best analysis result and choose "**Remove Original Recording Tempo and Analyze Again**". That new analysis will be saved to all other files in that group.
- ☑ Open the Smart Tempo Multitrack Set and only select the checkboxes for the files that you want to include in the analysis. Click **Update**.
- ☑ You can also bounce (BIP) the most relevant files for tempo detection and add the bounced files to the set. Now you can select that bounced file for the tempo detection (but mute it).

➡️ **... wait there is more**

And here are a few more changes regarding Smart Tempo and Flex:

- ☑ Flex settings for regions now update immediately after "**Remove Original Recording Tempo and Analyze Again**" is performed on them in the File Tempo Editor.

- ☑ *Double-clicking* the Ruler in the Smart Tempo Editor now starts playback at that location instead of the beginning of the current selection.

- ☑ The Smart Tempo Editor now shows the audio file waveform when selecting an audio region after a MIDI region has been selected.

- ☑ The "**Remove Original Recording Tempo from Audio File**" command now properly removes Flex Markers in cases where the command "**Remove Original Recording Tempo and Analyze Again**" has been executed before.

- ☑ In ADAPT Mode, trimming a region now removes tempo events in the range of the edit if no other regions exist in that range.

- ☑ In ADAPT Mode, exposing a portion of a recording performed during the count-in now creates the correct tempo for the newly revealed portion of the region.

- ☑ It is now possible to configure Logic Pro so that while Logic Pro is stopped, moving the playhead in the Smart Tempo Editor moves the playhead in the Main windows well.

- ☑ Smart Tempo analysis now shows a progress bar.

- ☑ The Insert Silence command now works reliably in ADAPT mode.

Add Photos to Note Pads

Basics

You can toggle the right window pane in Logic's Main Window to show the Note Pads ❶ with the following commands:

- 🎚️ **Click** on the Note Pads Button ❷ 🖼️ in the Control Bar
- 🎚️ Menu Command *View ➤ Show/Hide Note Pads*
- 🎚️ Key Command (*Show/Hide Note Pad*) ***opt+cmd+P***

➡️ *Project Note Pad and Track Note Pad*

The window pane has two taps, **Project** and **Track**. *Click* on them to to switch the view between the Project Note Pad ❸ and the Track Note Pad ❹.

🟡 Project Note Pad

This is the area where you can enter any notes about your Project.

🟡 Track Note Pad

- ▶ Each Track has its own Note Pad so you can enter information for each individual Track, for example, information about the artist you recorded, the used microphone, or notes for the mix.
- ▶ The Track Note Pad show the information of the currently selected Track.
- ▶ The text you enter in the Track Note Pad will also be displayed on the corresponding Channel Strip when you enabled the Channel Strip Component "Track Notes" ❺ in the Mixer.
- ▶ Technically, the Track Note Pad should be called "Channel Strip Note Pad" because that information is stored with the Channel Strip that is assigned to a Track and not with the Track itself. Assigning that Channel Strip to a different Track will move that notes with the Channel Strip to that Track.

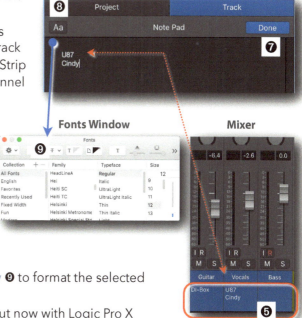

➡️ *Editing*

You can edit the text the following ways:

- ▶ *Click* on the **Edit** ❻ button (or ***double-click*** in the text area ❶) to switch to Edit Mode that lets you enter text in the text area. The button changed to a blue **Done** ❼ button. *Click* on it when finished entering text to exit Edit Mode.
- ▶ *Click* on the Font Button ❽ to open the Font Window ❾ to format the selected text.
- ▶ So far, you could only enter text into the Note Pad, but now with Logic Pro X 10.4.2, you can also add images to it.

➡️ **Adding Images**

Instead of writing what mic you used and add the description of how you placed the mic, you can take a picture ❶ and add that to the Note Pad. This is how it works:

▸ **Edit Mode**: You have to enter Edit Mode on the Note Pad by *clicking* the **Edit** button or *double-clicking* the text area

▸ **Drag and Drop**: You drag the image from the Finder directly onto the Note Pads area, as many as you want.

▸ **Inline With Text**: The image will be placed at the current Text Cursor where you moved it over with the mouse and then functions like an inline image that moves with the text.

▸ **Alpha Channel**: The Note Pad even supports alpha channel ❷ in an image.

▸ **Delete**: You delete an image by placing the Text Cursor to its right and press the **delete** key

➡️ **Image Formats**

Logic supports any of the standard image formats like png, jpeg, tiff, and even Animated GIFs (if you really want to have fun with it).

➡️ **Editing Images**

The new image implementation goes even one step further and lets you edit the image right inside Logic.

☑ Switch to Edit Mode by *clicking* the **Edit** ❸ button or *double-clicking* the text area

☑ When you move the mouse cursor over the image in the Note Pads, a downward arrow ❹ appears in the upper right corner of the image.

☑ *Click* on that arrow (Action Button) and a popup menu appears with the menu item Markup

☑ *Click* on **Markup** ❺ to open the image in the Markup window ❻.

☑ You can use any of the tools ❼ in that window to alter the image, add annotations or objects, or crop the image. This is the same macOS tool available to other apps like the Mail app. Here are more information about it https://support.apple.com/guide/mail/mark-up-attachments-mlhl98889a61/mac

☑ *Click* the **Done** ❽ button to close the window with those changes.

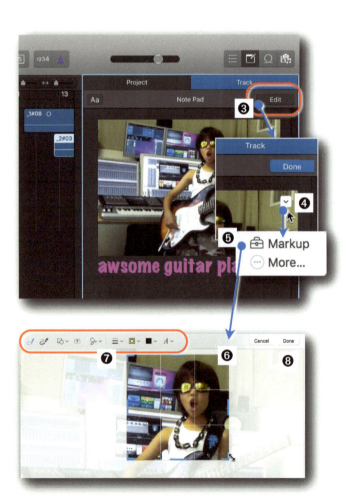

Control Bar

Count-In Button with Popup Menu

Control Bar

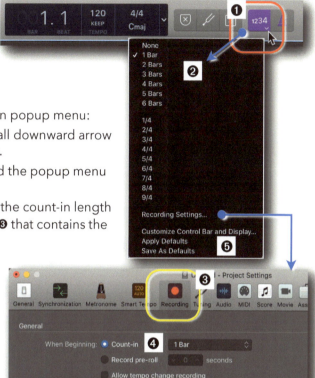

The Count-In Button ❶ on the Control Bar now has its own popup menu:

▶ When you move the mouse over the button, a small downward arrow appears that indicates that there is a popup menu.

▶ *Long-click*, *right-click*, or *ctr+click* on the button and the popup menu opens ❷.

▶ The popup menu contains the various options for the count-in length plus a command to open the Recording Settings. ❸ that contains the same options ❹.

▶ The three commands ❺ at the bottom of the menu are the same that are available when *ctr+clicking* on the Control Bar background.

Toolbar

Toolbar Button "Keyswitches" changed to "Articulation"

The previous Toolbar Button **"Keyswitches"** ❻ has been renamed to **"Articulation"** ❼ with a new icon. The checkbox in the Toolbar Configuration Popover has been renamed accordingly ❽.

Right-click below Track Headers

It is now possible to *right-click* on the blank area ❶ below the last Track in the Track List to open a Shortcut Menu ❷. The menu items are a subset of the Shortcut Menu ❸ that opens when *right-clicking* on a Track Header ❹.

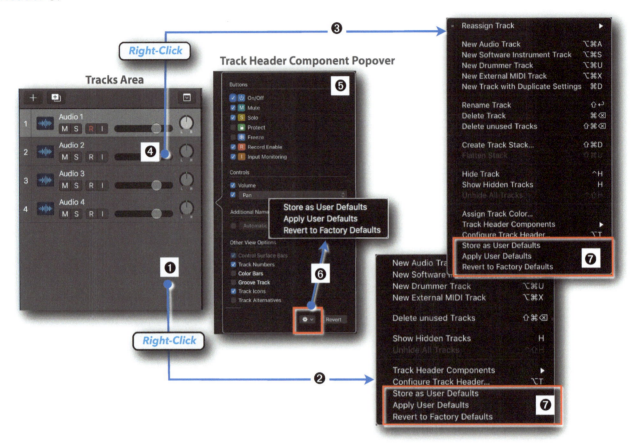

"Defaults" Commands available in the Shortcut Menu

When you open the Track Header Component Configuration Popover ❺ (*opt+T*), you see at the bottom the Action Button ⚙⌄ ❻ that opens a menu with three commands **Store User Defaults**, **Apply User Defaults**, and **Revert to Factory Defaults** that determine the configuration of the Track Header Components. Now, these commands are also available at the bottom of the Shortcut Menus ❼.

More Changes and Improvements in the Tracks Area

➡️ **Track Stacks**

- ☑ Selecting a Summing Stack's header now reliably selects all regions inside the Stack in cases where it contains Folder Stacks.
- ☑ The shaded area beneath an open Track Stack in the Tracks area now changes color immediately when the color of the Track Stack Aux is changed.

➡️ **Global Tracks**

- ☑ *Clicking* on a Marker no longer sometimes unexpectedly creates another short Marker at the same position.
- ☑ Moving an Arrange Marker now correctly repositions all regions when there is a Groove Master track controlling a phase locked edit group.
- ☑ The first signature in the Signature Track is now selected as expected when the track is opened with Cycle enabled.

➡️ **Track List**

- ☑ It is now possible to abort renaming a track by pressing **Esc**.
- ☑ The contextual menu to rename a track now works when a plug-in window has focus.
- ☑ Scroll bars in the Track List now immediately update when dragging objects from the Environment to the Track list to create new tracks.
- ☑ Pressing the down arrow now moves the cursor to the end of the text when editing a track name.
- ☑ Undo now works after changing a track color.

Sh+double-click on Workspace to start Playback

Logic Pro X v10.4 introduced the feature to *sh+click* anywhere on the Workspace (not a Region) to place the Playhead at that position. Now you can *sh+double-click* on the Workspace (and the Piano Roll Editor and Score Editor) to place the Playhead at that position and start the playback ... nice!

Help Tag for Nudging Regions

The *Preferences ➤ Display ➤ General* has a checkbox **Show Help Tags ❶**. When enabled, a Help Tag ❷ in the form of a little black window (a popover with an "anchor" pointing at the object) will appear when moving Regions, MIDI Events, or Automation Control Points in the Workspace or the MIDI Editors. It provides information about that specific action (move, copy, trim, etc.).

Now that Help Tag will also be displayed when nudging a Region in the Workspace
   Key Command *opt+ArrowLeft/Right* (or any of the many Nudge Key Commands)
   Click on the Nudge Button ❸ on the Toolbar.

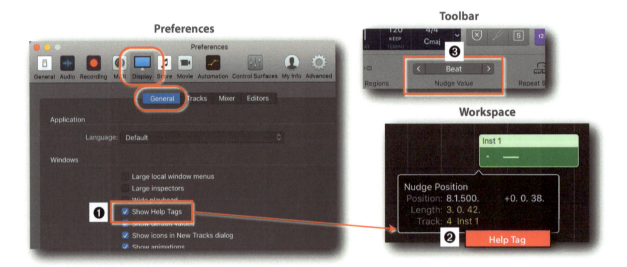

Help Tag when drawing Marquee Selection

A Help Tag ❹ is now also displayed when *dragging* a Marquee Selection ❺.

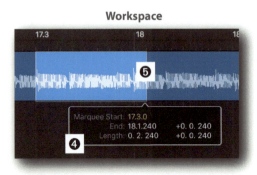

Sh+opt+click extends other end of Marquee Selection

Logic added another click action to adjust the length of a Marquee Selection.

▶ **Extend Marquee Selection**: So far, if you have an existing Marquee Selection and want to extend or shorten the left or right border, you *sh+click* on that area. If you are closer to the left border ❶, then that side of the border is affected and if you are closer to the right border ❷, then that side is affected.

▶ **Extend Marquee Selection (opposite side)**: Now Logic adds another click variation (similar to Markers). *Sh+opt+clicking* close to the left border (inside the selection) will shorten the right border ❸, and *sh+opt+clicking* close to the right border (inside the selection) will shorten the left border ❹ of the Marquee Selection

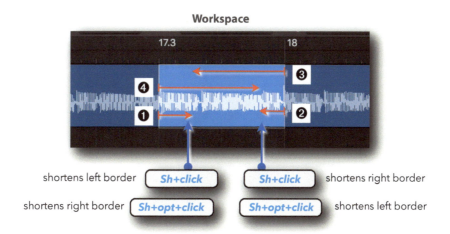

Workspace

shortens left border   **Sh+click**   **Sh+click**   shortens right border

shortens right border   **Sh+opt+click**   **Sh+opt+click**   shortens left border

Boxed ProgramChange Number in MIDI Region

The MIDI Region on the Workspace now display any ProgramChange ❺ Events as a boxed number ❻.

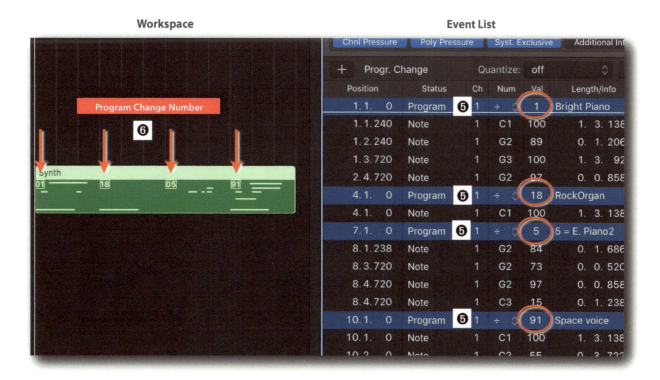

Workspace   Event List

Join Looped MIDI Region

In 10.4.1, if you have a looped MIDI Region ❶, you couldn't convert the entire length with all the loop iterations to a single MIDI Region. The only way was to use the **Convert Loops to Regions** ❷ command and then join (*cmd+J*) those Regions together.

Now in 10.4.2, you can use the Join Regions command (*cmd+J*) to convert the looped Region to a single Region ❸.

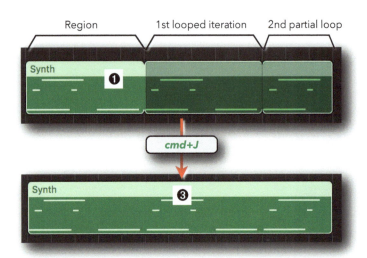

Region Shortcut Menu

Remove Silence: "Threshold" value in dB

You can open the Remove Silence Dialog by selecting the Audio Region and choosing any of the following commands:

 Key Command *ctr+X*

 Tracks Area Local Menu *Functions ➤ Remove Silence from Audio Region...*

 Audio Track Editor Local Menu *Functions ➤ Remove Silence from Audio Region...*

The **Threshold** value that was displayed in **%** ❹ in 10.4.1 is now displayed in **dB** ❺.

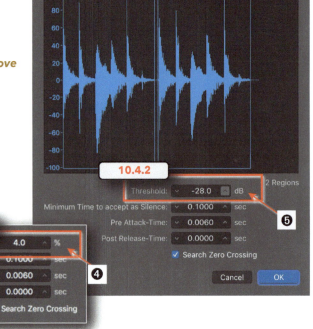

Remove Silence Dialog

One Recording Mode renamed to "Create New Track"

The name of the command for the Overlapping Audio Recording Mode ❶ has been changed from **Create Track** ❷ to **Create New Track** ❸.

The name has also been updated accordingly in the popup menu *Preferences ➤ Recording* ❹.

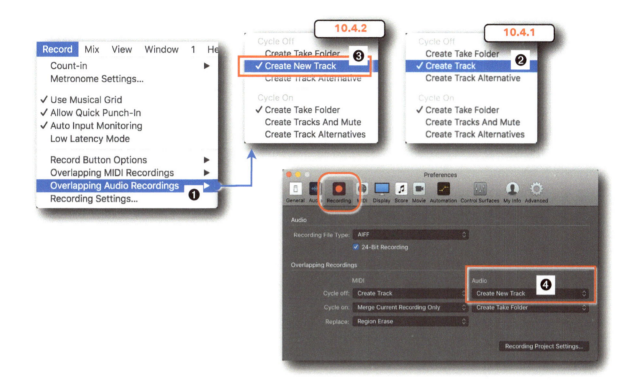

Add Selected Files as Stems

When you *right-click* on multiple selected Audio Files ❺ in the Project Audio Browser or *drag* files onto the Workspace (from the Project Audio Browser, the All Files Browser, or the Finder ❻), the Add Selected Files to Tracks Dialog ❼ opens with a new checkbox **All selected files are stems from one project** ❽. Please note that this checkbox is not displayed when **Place all files on one track** ❾ above is selected.

I demonstrated that important checkbox with all its "consequences" in the chapter about Smart Tempo.

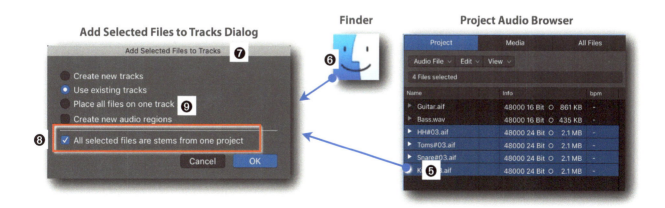

QuickSwipe Comping disables Catch Playhead

The Catch Playhead ❶ status will automatically disabled when editing a Take Folder using any of the QuickSwipe operations ❷.

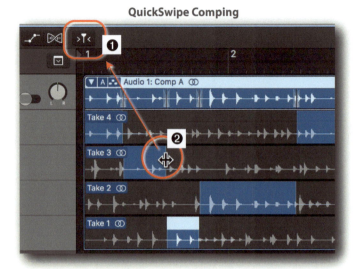

QuickSwipe Comping

Hidden Marquee Tool Function

There is a line in the 10.4.2 release notes about the following fix: "**Command-Shift clicking to adjust Marquee selections again works as expected**". I guess most Logic users don't know about this hidden feature (including me, I just found out recently). Here is how it works:

▶ When you draw a Marquee Selection ❸, you create a rectangle that determines the time information (from left border to right border ❹) and the Track information (which Track Lanes ❺ are included/selected) for that selection.

▶ The Marquee Selection includes adjacent Tracks. However, that doesn't have to be that way!

▶ You can *sh+click* on a Track Lane to remove ❻ or add ❼ that Track Lane to the Marquee Selection (with the same left and right border ❹). Be aware that the release note lists the modifier key "**command-shift**", however, this assumes that the Command-Tool is assigned to the Marquee Tool. If you have the Marquee Tool already selected, then you just hold down the shift key.

▶ Use the same *shift-click* (or *sh-cmd-click*) action to extend the left or right border of the selection.

▶ Pro Tools users might recognize this functionality which is similar to the "Edit Selection" in Pro Tools.

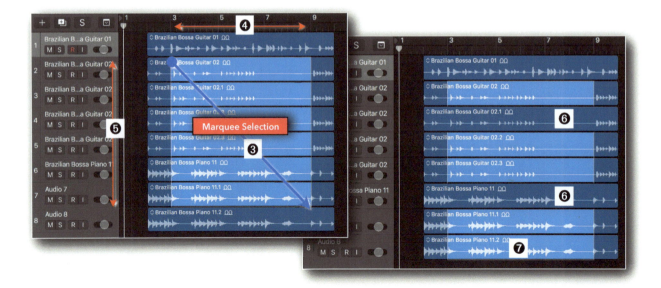

More Editing Improvements

➡ *Regions*

- ☑ **_Shift-double-clicking_** a region again selects all regions on the same Track in cases where Automation is not being displayed, and the "Quick Swipe and Take Editing click zones" preference is enabled.
- ☑ When adjusting multiple selected Loops on different tracks, the lengths of all selected Loops are again set correctly when dragging a loop other than the topmost in the selection.
- ☑ Solo playing a Region in the Audio Track Editor now always plays the entire region, even if there is a Marquee selection in the Tracks area.
- ☑ After recording MIDI over an existing region using the Merge recording option, the "Discard recording" key command no longer discards both the new recording and the original region.

➡ *Apple Loops*

- ☑ **_Dragging_** yellow Drummer Loops into the Track Area now creates a Channel Strip with the volume set to match the Preview volume setting in the Loop Browser.
- ☑ **_Dragging_** loops that do not contain a **Genre** or **Instrument** tag into the Loop Browser now trigger an alert indicating they should be added as Untagged Loops.

➡ *QuickSwipe Comping*

- ☑ Loading a new Patch that creates a Summing Stack on an Audio Track with an open Take Folder no longer sometimes causes the track to disappear from view in the Tracks Area when the Mixer is in Tracks view.
- ☑ QuickSwipe Comping during playback no longer sometimes interrupts playback of the Take folder.
- ☑ QuickSwipe Comping during playback now disables Catch Playhead Position.
- ☑ Catch Playhead mode is now disabled while editing Takes during playback.
- ☑ Copying a Take region inside a Take Folder no longer resets the original region settings to defaults.

➡ *Fades*

- ☑ After using Control+Shift to add a fade to a region, it is again deselected as expected.
- ☑ Fade Outs are no longer sometimes dimmed on Flexed regions.
- ☑ It is again possible to create short crossfades with the Crossfade tool at low zoom settings.
- ☑ Fades are now reliably applied to all tracks in an editing group.

Lasso Around Automation Points

The visual feedback for selecting Automation Control Points on the Automation Lane by dragging around them (aka "lasso-around" or "rubber-band") has been slightly improved and now makes more sense:

⬤ *Select Control Points on x-axis (drag)*

With this procedure, you just *drag* left-right ❶ on the Automation Lane, and all Automation Control Points in that range will be selected when you release the mouse ❷.

Prior to v10.4.2, when you dragged on an area, you would draw a box on the Automation Lane that increased/decreased, depending on how far you dragged horizontally and vertically, even though the vertical position was not relevant.

Now when you drag, you only move the left or right border ❸ of the entire selection on the Automation Lane, similar to a Marquee Selection. When you release the mouse, the shaded range disappears, and all the Control Points inside that selection are selected ❷.

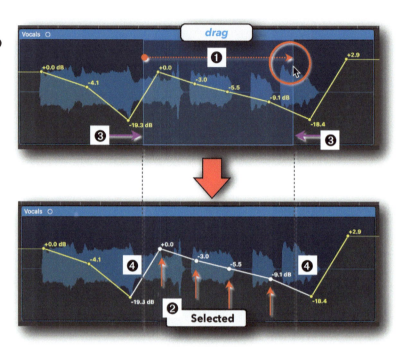

> ▶ **Control Point vs. Line Segment**
>
> Please note that the line segment left and right of a selected Control Point is selected (white). That's why it seems that the Control Points ❹ outside the dragged range were also selected. However, if you look closely, you can see that only the selected Control Points turned white.

Remember that you can also *drag* a range across adjacent Tracks (displaying the same Automation Parameter).

⬤ *Select Control Pint on x/y-axis (opt-drag)*

This feature was introduced in Logic Pro X 10.4 where you *opt+drag* around Control Points ❺. Now you control the size of the box you are drawing, based on the vertical and horizontal position of your mouse cursor, and only the Control Points inside that box will be selected ❻ when you release the mouse.

This feature is useful if you only want to adjust the higher or lower values of an Automation Curve, or a range in-between.

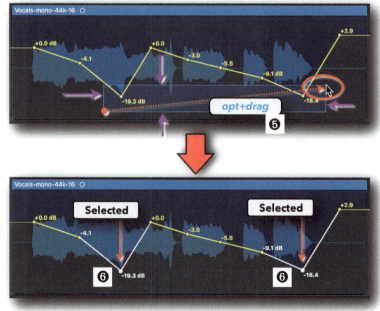

This new Automation feature is very subtle, and you have to look closely to notice its effect. I demonstrate the effect with four screenshots:

🟡 *Screenshot #1*

The example shows an Automation Curve for the Automation Parameter **Volume** with four Automation Control Points ❶ on the Automation Lane.

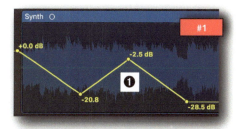

🟡 *Screenshot #2*

I *click-hold* on the third Control Point and *drag* it to the left ❷.

☑ The Control Point is selected, turning white and the line segment before and after the Control Point also turns white.

☑ A thin white vertical Alignment Guide ❸ appears, spanning from the Ruler on top vertically across the entire Workspace. It marks the position of the Control Point and moves along horizontally while you are dragging the Control Point

☑ A Help Tag ❹ appears, pointing with its "anchor" at the current drag position. It follows that position while moving and displays the current **Position** value of the Control Point and its value, in this case, the **Volume**.

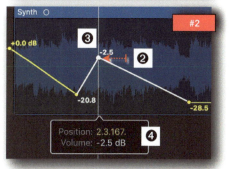

🟡 *Screenshot #3*

This is the new behavior in 10.4.2

Prior to v10.4.2, when you drag a Control Point over an existing Control Point, it automatically removes it (although it will reappear if you drag back while still pressing down the mouse button).

Now in v10.4.2 when you reach the position of the adjacent Control Point, it will first snap to that position, so both Control Points are at the same position ❺. Be careful, you have to move slowly to that position or you will "overshoot" it and delete the existing Control Point.

If you open the Track Automation Event List (only available as a Key Command *ctr+opt+E*), you can see that both Control Points have the same position ❻.

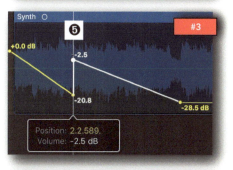

Track Automation Event List

L	M	Position	Status	Ch	Num	Val	Length/Info
		1.1. 0	F	1	7	90	Volume
		1.4.866.	F	1	7	90	Volume
❻		2.2.589.	F	1	7	27	Volume
		2.2.589.	F	1	7	77	Volume
		3.1.455.	F	1	7	17	Volume

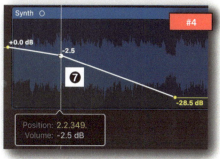

🟡 *Screenshot #4*

When you *drag* further and move over the existing Control Point, it will be removed ❼.
Remember, it will reappear if you drag back while still pressing down the mouse button.

More Automation Improvements and Bug Fixes

Here are a few more improvements for Automation:

- ☑ It is now possible to use the Pencil Tool to *draw* region automation in the Tracks area at small horizontal zoom settings.
- ☑ Automation display no longer switches unexpectedly to Volume when the command "**Create 2 Automation Points for Visible Parameter**" is used with **Autoselect Automation Parameter in Read Mode** enabled.
- ☑ The **Cycle Through Used Parameters** command in the Piano Roll now only shows Region-based Automation parameters contained in the currently selected region.
- ☑ CC#7 messages automated for the Access Virus T1 plug-in now reliably can be set to any value from 0 to 127.
- ☑ Grouped tracks now reliably maintain their correct relative automation levels when automation is adjusted for one of them using the Track header trim control.
- ☑ The Automation Menu again consistently shows all parameters for plug-ins that offer between 29-46 parameters.
- ☑ Display of Region-based Automation on MIDI regions in the Tracks area now immediately updates when selecting events in the Event List.

Articulation Set Editor

"Tab" Key to rename Articulations

In the **Articulations** view ❶ of the Articulation Set Editor you can now press the **tab** key to select the name field ❷ of the currently selected Articulation to enter a new name. Pressing the **tab** key again will select the name field of the next Articulation on that list.

Articulation Set Editor

Activate Multiple Outputs

The **Output** view ❸ of the Articulation Set Editor has a new checkbox **Activate Multiple Outputs** ❹ at the bottom of the window. When enabled, it adds two more rows ❺ to each Articulation row, so Logic can send up to three MIDI Messages for each defined Articulation to Instrument Plugins.

Articulation Set Editor

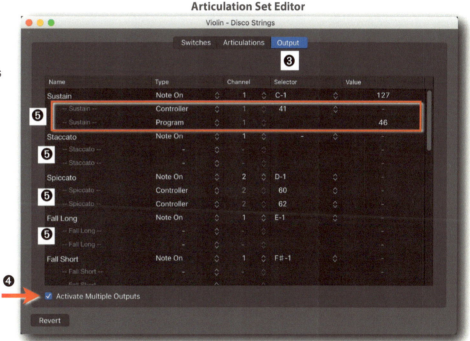

New Key Command to "Open Articulation Editor"

There is now a new Key Command "**Open Articulation Editor**" ❻.

Please note that you have to select a Track that has an Articulation assigned to it in the Track Inspector, so the Key Command knows which Articulation Editor to open.

Key Command Window

Removed "Settings" Option from Articulation Set Menu

Clicking the Articulation Set ❶ parameter in the Track Inspector will open the Articulation Set Menu ❷.

That menu previously had a "useless" header **Settings** ❸ that is not displayed anymore.

As you can see on the screenshot, any assigned Key Equivalent for the new Key Command "**Open Articulation Editor**" will be displayed next to the menu item **Edit…** . Here I use *sh+ctr+E* ❹.

Alert Dialog when overwriting existing Articulation Setting File

When you use the **Save As…** ❺ command from the Articulation Set Menu, a Save Dialog opens with the *~/Music/Audio Music Apps/Articulation Settings/* ❻ directory pre-selected. This is the place where you store your user Articulation Settings. When you enter a name ❼ that already exists in this folder, a Warning Dialog ❽ pops up that you have to confirm.

In previous versions, the existing file was overwritten immediately without a dialog.

Setting the Default Articulation from the Local Inspector

The Local Inspector on the left side of the Piano Roll Editor ❶ and Score Editor ❷ has an Articulation Selector ❸ that opens a menu ❹ with the available Articulations to choose from (make sure to increase the height of the Editor to display all components).

So far, the selector provided two functionalities:

☑ **Display Note Articulation**: When you select one or multiple notes ❺ in the Editor, then the selector ❸ will display the Articulation of those notes. Please note that if the selected notes have different Articulations assigned to them, then the selector will display an asterisk (*).

☑ **Select Note Articulation**: When one or multiple notes are selected in the Editor, then selecting an Articulation from the menu ❹ of the Articulation Selector will assign that Articulation to all currently selected notes.

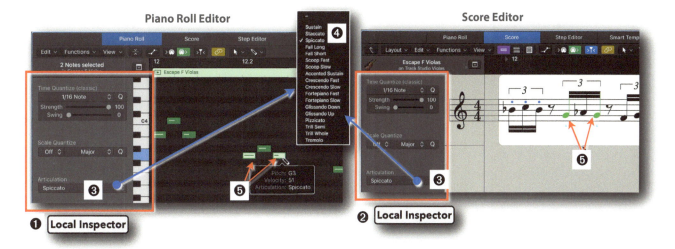

Now in 10.4.2, the selector has a third function:

☑ **Set Default Articulation**: If no Note Events are selected ❻ in the Editor, then choosing an Articulation from the Articulation Menu ❼ will switch the current Default Articulation for that Instrument to the one you select in the menu. You can verify that, for example, if you have the Plugin Window open and its Articulation Selector ❽ visible.

Toolbar Button "Keyswitches" is now "Articulation"

The previous Toolbar Button **"Keyswitches"** ❶ has been renamed to **"Articulation"** ❷ with a new icon. The checkbox in the Toolbar Configuration Popover has been renamed accordingly ❸.

Remember that his switch toggles the functionality, whether incoming MIDI Messages are used as Articulation Switches (as configured in the current Articulation Set). This **Articulation** ❹ button is linked to the **"MIDI Remote"** button in the Smart Controls ❺ and the Articulation Set Editor. Please review the in-depth information about that Articulation routing concept in my book "Logic Pro X - What's New in 10.4".

Smart Control Window

MIDI Preferences

Articulation Improvements

There are a few more fixes and improvements regarding the Articulations:

- ☑ Muted notes no longer unexpectedly send their articulations to key switches.
- ☑ Notes without Articulation IDs are no longer treated as having Articulation ID 1.
- ☑ Pressing **Enter** no longer sometimes causes the Articulation Set window to unexpectedly lose focus.
- ☑ When the MIDI Preference ❻ for MIDI Remote is set to **Per Channel Strip** ❼, the Articulations switch in the Toolbar ❹ now updates its status depending on whether MIDI Remote is active for articulations on the current track.
- ☑ CC events recorded to a track with an Articulation set loaded no longer have an articulation ID unexpectedly attached.
- ☑ When multiple regions with different articulation sets are selected, it is no longer possible to inadvertently apply an articulation from a different region to a note.

Automatic Slur

A Slur is a curved line ❶ between two or more notes to instruct a legato playing style (single bow, single breath, single pick, etc.).

➡ *Manual Slurs vs. Automatic Slurs*

A few differences between the Manual Slurs and the Automatic Slurs:

▶ Automatic Slurs look the same as Manual Slurs in the Score Editor and can only be distinguished by their behavior when editing them.

▶ Manual Slurs are placed as graphical objects (Events) on the Score Editor and adjusted to determine over which notes they are placed on. Automatic Slurs are placed by defining the first and last note.

Manual Slur

▶ Manual Slurs are discrete Events that are displayed in the Event List ❷, but not Automatic Slurs.

▶ Manual Slurs show Guide Lines ❸ for the position on the staff; Automatic Slurs automatically snap to the corresponding note.

▶ Automatic Slurs can only be attached to selected notes of the same Voice.

▶ Slurs in an imported MusicXML file will become Manual Slurs.

▶ Slurs cannot be extended beyond Region borders.

▶ Joining Regions will automatically extend or join existing Slurs.

▶ Unlike Manual Slurs, Automatic Slurs will follow any transposition, or when copy/moving notes that have attachedAutomatic Slurs.

➡ *Part Box*

The Crescendo and Slurs Group ❹ in the Part Box of the Main Inspector has the new symbol, the Automatic Slur icon ❺ ⌒. *Dragging* it over notes in the Score Editor will create Automatic Slur(s).

Part Box

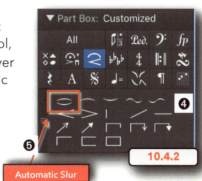

Part Box

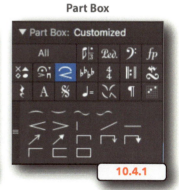

➡️ Shortcut Menu

Right-click on a note ❶ in the Score Editor to open its Shortcut Menu. It now has a new submenu for the Automatic Slurs ❷.

- **Convert to Manual Slur**: Converts the Automatic Slur to a Manual Slur. Manual Slurs cannot be converted to Automatic Slurs.
- **Slur Above**: Places the Slur above the notes.
- **Slur Below**: Places the Slur below the notes.
- **Slur Auto Direction**: Logic chooses the above or below placement.
- **Settings: Extended Layout**: Opens the *Project Settings ➤ Score ➤ Layout*
- **Reset Slur**: Removes any manual adjustments of the Automatic Slur and resets it to its default position.

You can also **right-click** on the Slur itself to open its own Shortcut Menu ❸ with the Automatic Slur options plus two additional commands (if you **right-clic**k on a Slur and it doesn't open a Shortcut Menu, then it is a Manual Slur).

- **Slur Last Note**: Use this command to break up a long Slur into smaller "sections".
- **Slur(s) for non-contiguous selected notes**: Create Slurs by only selecting the first and last note of that group.

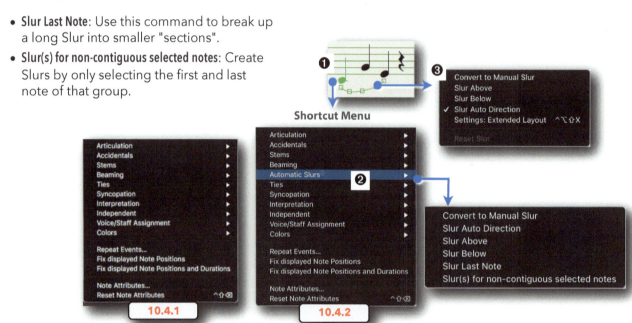

➡️ Local Functions Menu

The Local Functions Menu ❹ in the Score Editor has a submenu for the Note Attributes ❺. It contains a new submenu for the Automatic Slurs ❻. with the same commands as the Shortcut Menus.

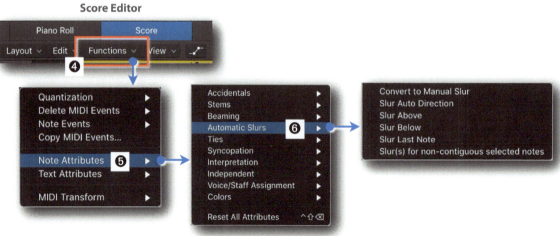

5 - Editors

➡️ **Creating/Editing Slurs**

The advantage of using Automatic Slurs is speed and ease of use. You can just drag the symbol over a note or a group of notes, and the Slurs are automatically applied based on the selected notes, and the layout preferences. You can apply Slurs in three different ways:

- *Drag* the Slur Symbol over a note (or selected notes)
- Use a Menu Command on selected notes
- Use a Key Command on selected notes

🟡 **Dragging the Symbol**

Here are the rules when dragging the Automatic Slur Symbol 〰️ from the Part Box onto the Score Editor:

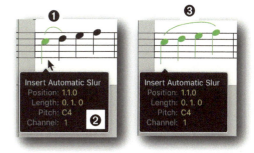

▸ *Dragging* the symbol over a note that is not selected will add an Automatic Slur between that note and the following note ❶. A Help Tag ❷ appears with information about the drag position.

▸ *Dragging* the symbol over a group of selected notes will add a single Automatic Slur over all the selected notes ❸.

▸ If you have multiple notes selected ❹ (contiguous and non-contiguous), then dragging over one of the selected notes will add individual Automatic Slurs ❺ to all groups of selected notes. Any single selected note will have an Automatic Slur selected between that note and its following note.

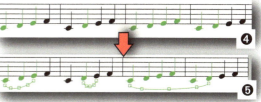

🟡 **Pencil Tool**

You can also use the Pencil Tool ✎ to add Automatic Slurs graphically.

- *Click* with the Pencil Tool on a note or selected notes to create an Automatic Slur between that note and the following note.
- *Click-hold* on a note and *drag* over adjacent notes to determine the range for the newly created Automatic Slur.

Slur(s) for non-contiguous selected notes

🟡 **Command**

Here are some of the commands that are available in the Shortcut Menus and the local Functions Menu:

Slur(s) for non-contiguous selected notes

▸ Using the Slur command (**Slur Auto Direction**, **Slur Above**, and **Slur Below**) on a single note will add a Slur between that note and the following note (even if there is a rest in between).

▸ Using the command on a group of selected notes ❹ will apply Automatic Slur(s) to any group ❺ of selected notes.

▸ The command **Slur(s) for non-contiguous selected notes** will add a Slur ❻ between the first selected note and the next selected note, including all the unselected ("non-contiguous") notes in between.

▸ With multiple selected notes, the command **Slur(s) for non-contiguous selected notes** will "slur" individually from one selected to the next selected, and if there are unselected notes in between, then they are included ❼.

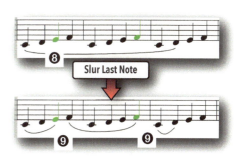

Slur Last Note

▸ You can break up a single Slur ❽ (a group of notes) into smaller groups with the command **Slur Last Note**. Select the note (or notes) to mark the last note of the new group of notes ❾.

● Key Commands

Most Automatic Slur commands are also available as Key Commands ❶, but they are not assigned by default.

Key Command Window

● Edit Slurs

There are several ways to edit Automatic Slurs:

▶ **Length**: *Drag* the start and end handle of the Slur to shorten or lengthen the Slur. While dragging the Slur, it will snap to the corresponding note.

▶ **Shape**: *Drag* the other handles of the Slur curve to change the shape of the Slur.

▶ **Delete**: *Click* on the Slur and press the delete key.

➡ Score Project Settings

The **Project Settings ➤ Score ➤ Layout** ❷ page has four new layout parameters for the Automatic Slurs ❸.

Score Project Settings

Other Score Editor Improvements and Bug Fixes

Here is a list of other improvements and bug fixes in the Score Editor:

- ☑ Inserting symbols into the Score now works when multiple Projects are open.
- ☑ The Score again reliably displays the correct colors when coloring notes by pitch.
- ☑ Crescendo/decrescendo symbols now reliably display in the correct positions when switching the score from full score view to part display.
- ☑ Switching from the Smart Controls editor to the Main Window Score Editor with Automation showing no longer causes the Staff to be hidden.
- ☑ Drum staves now reliably display correctly with looped regions.
- ☑ Brackets for connected staves now reliably display in linear Score view.
- ☑ It is again possible to insert the Arrow Up slur symbol in the Score.
- ☑ In the Drum.0 Clef style, the ":" repeat sign now displays at the correct position.
- ☑ Inserted chord symbols now reliably remain visible in cases where more than 8 chords have been inserted in the same bar.

Piano Roll Editor

Articulation Name in Help Tag

The Help Tag that pops up in the Piano Roll Editor when editing MIDI Note Events (the Note Bars), now also display the name of the Articulation ❶ assigned to that Note Event.

The Help Tag will not only appear when you *drag* the Note Bar or its borders but also when you just move the mouse over a Note Bar ❷. Of course, the **Show Help Tags** ❸ checkbox has to be enabled in the *Preferences ➤ Display ➤ General* for the Help Tag to be displayed.

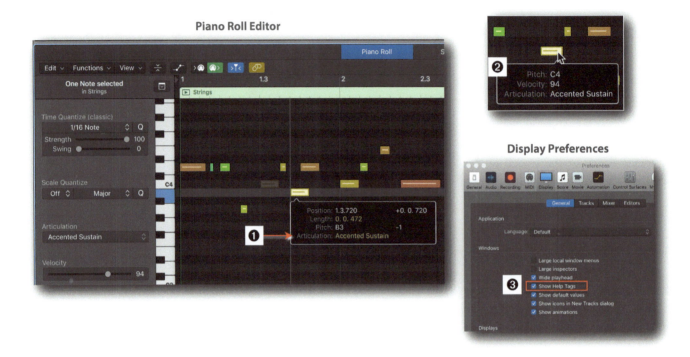

Piano Roll Editor

Other Piano Roll Editor Improvements

- ☑ The visible area in the Piano Roll can now be scrolled with the mouse wheel or touch pad.
- ☑ It is now only possible to disable link mode in the Piano Roll if there is at least one region selected.
- ☑ The view in the Piano Roll no longer unexpectedly jumps to the project start when scrolling after zooming in to a single note.
- ☑ Data pasted from the Piano Roll to the Tracks area now is consistently placed at the correct position.
- ☑ The view in the Piano Roll now jumps correctly to the left edge of the cycle zone when playing in Cycle mode.
- ☑ Notes copied from the Piano Roll and then pasted to the Tracks area no longer cause the Playheads to move to the wrong position.
- ☑ Pasted MIDI data is no longer unexpectedly offset in region where the left corner has been trimmed.

Mixer

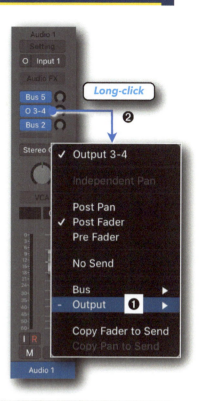

Route Sends to Outputs

In Logic 10.4.1 you could only use the Sends to route the signal to any of the 256 Busses. Now in 10.4.2, you can also route a Send to one of the available Output Channels, for example, to create a separate Mix or use it in multitrack configurations to create a parallel stereo downmix.

Attention

The **Output** ❶ submenu in the Sends Menu ❷ will only be displayed if your currently selected Audio Interface has more than 2 channels.

Single-Click on VCA Slot to open Popup Menu

Here is a change to the VCA Slot on the Channel Strip:

▶ **10.4.1**: You had to *right-click* or *long-click* on the VCA Slot ❸ to open its popup menu ❹.

▶ **10.4.2**: Now you just *click* on the VCA Slot, and the popup menu opens.

Attention

Unfortunately, the other strange click behaviors are still in place on the Channel Strip:

☑ **Channel Mote Button**: *Click* on the Channel Mode Button ❺ to toggle between Mono ⚪ and Stereo ⚭. You have to *right-click* to open the Channel Mode Menu ❻ to access all five Channel Format (Mono ⚪, Stereo ⚭, Left ⚭, Right ⚭, Surround ⊞)

☑ **Sends Button**: You can *click* on an empty Send Slot ❼ and the Sends Menu opens. However, once a Send was assigned, and the blue Send Button ❽ appeared, you have to *long-click* (not *right-click*) on the button to open the menu ❾.

☑ **Output Button**: You have to *right-click* or *long-click* the Output Button ❿ to open its popup menu.

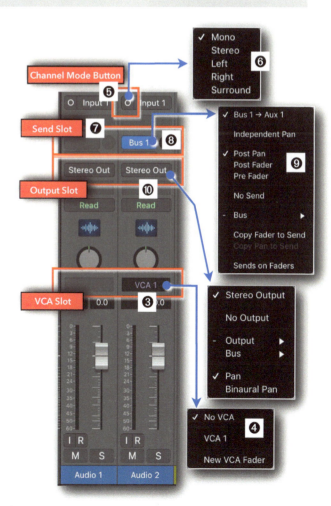

Special Cmd+click on Menu Command in Send Menu

Clicking on the Send Button ❶ of a Channel Strip opens the Sends Menu ❷ with various menu commands, for example, to select the Bus for that send, set the Pre/Post status, or select the Independent Pan option.

When holding down the **command** key when clicking on any of those commands will apply that command to the Sends on any Channel Strip routed to that same Bus. The Send can be on any Send Slot and the Channel Strips don't have to be selected first.

This is a quick way to reroute Sends from one Bus ❸ to a different Bus ❹ to quickly send them to a different Aux Return or to enable the Independent Pan on all Sends routed to a specific Bus.

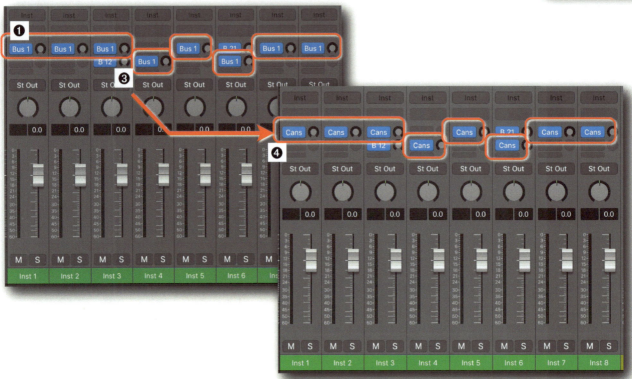

KC "Add Selected Channel Strips to Selected Group"

A new Key Command **Add Selected Channel Strips to Selected Groups** ❻ lets you add all the currently selected Channel Strips (or Tracks in the Tracks Area) directly to the selected Channel Strip Group(s) without using the command ❼ from the Action Menu ❽ in the Group Inspector.

Correct Volume Display with Negative Values

The Volume Display ❶ is the little number display above the Volume Fader on a Channel Strip that shows the position of the Volume Fader. The problem with this display before 10.4.2 was that it omitted the minus sign if you set the Fader to -10dB or below, displaying an incorrect number ❷. Now in 10.4.2, the minus sign is properly displayed ❸.

However, when you select the Volume Display (so it has key focus ❹) to position the Volume Fader numerically, it still isn't perfect, because now, the decimal value is not displayed together with the number.

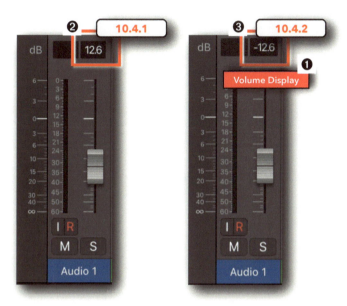 

Improvements and Bug Fixes

Here are a few more Improvements and Bug Fixes in the Mixer:

Improvements

- ☑ The **Select Members** command in the Groups window action menu now selects all tracks assigned to channel strips that are part of the group.
- ☑ A Track removed from a group is no longer controlled by that group unless the group is first disabled and then re-enabled.
- ☑ A selected Software Instrument track now continues to respond to MIDI input after an audio loop is dragged into the Tracks area.

Bug Fixes

- ☑ Choosing "**Create new tracks for the regions you are about to paste**" when pasting regions into the Tracks area no longer sometimes creates non-functioning channel strips in the Mixer.
- ☑ Pasting "**Plug-ins Only**" from a factory Software Instrument channel strip setting to an empty Software Instrument channel strip no longer also pastes the name.
- ☑ Changing the order of automation lanes on a track assigned to an Aux no longer causes the output assignment of the Aux to be changed to match the input Bus.
- ☑ Inserting Multi-mono Plugins on an Instrument track set to surround no longer produces unexpected feedback in certain rare cases.

Space Designer

"Reverb Output" renamed to "Wet Output"

The **Wet** ❶ parameter of the Space Designer Plugin has its Automation Parameter ❷ renamed from "**Reverb Output**" ❸ to the more proper name "**Wet Output**" ❹

Modifier / Scripter

Change Scale in 1% Increments

Moving the slider ❺ of the **Scale** parameter in the Modifier Plugin (MIDI FX) now changes in 1% increments instead of 10% increments.

This also applied to the Scripter Plugin.

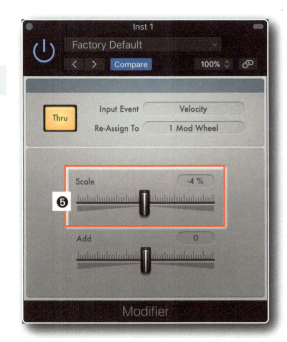

ChromaVerb

New Command "Reset Damping EQ"

In the **MAIN** view of the ChromaVerb *right-click* on the label **Damping EQ** ❶ in the upper-left corner Plugin Window, and a Shortcut Menu opens with a single command "**Reset Damping EQ**" ❷. This command will reset ("flatten") the curve of the Damping EQ ❸.

New Command "Reset Output EQ"

In the **DETAILS** view of the ChromaVerb *right-click* on the label **Output EQ** ❹ on top of the Plugin Window, and a Shortcut Menu opens with a single command "**Reset Output EQ**" ❺. This command will reset ("flatten") the curve of the Damping EQ ❻.

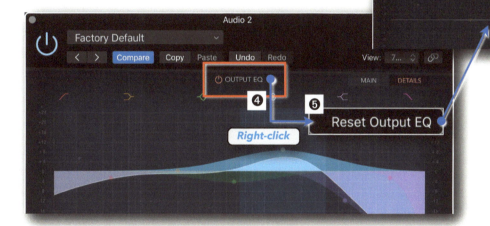

Visualization Status saved with Presets

The Main View has a Visualization Button ❼ in the lower-right corner that lets you enable the cool graphics, representing the energy distribution of the reverb signal. The status of that Visualization Button (on/off) is now saved and restored with Plug-In Preset.

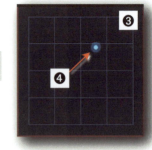

Step FX and Phat FX

New Visual FX

Both Audio FX Plugins, Step FX ❶ and Phat FX ❷ have an XY Pad ❸ with a blue puck ❹ that you can move to change the two parameters assigned to X and Y simultaneously.

That blue puck now has an animated effect around it that responds to the processed signal ❺. This is more of an eye candy than a useful feature. But why not, it doesn't have to be cat videos all the time to get distracted when working in Logic.

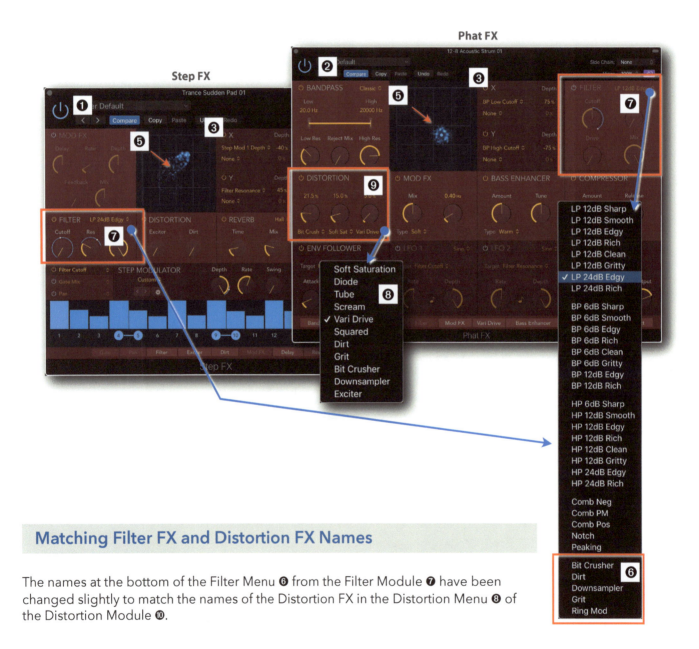

Matching Filter FX and Distortion FX Names

The names at the bottom of the Filter Menu ❻ from the Filter Module ❼ have been changed slightly to match the names of the Distortion FX in the Distortion Menu ❽ of the Distortion Module ❿.

Enter Parameter Values Numerically

Now you **double-click** on the label ❶ of any parameter in the **ADVANCED** view, and a white entry box ❷ opens where you can enter the parameter value numerically. Press enter or **click** outside that field to enter that value.

Indicator for Enabled Source Filter

In the ADVANCED ❸ view, when selecting any of the Sources **A**, **B**, **C**, **D** ❹ on the left side, you see the Filter section ❺ with three Filter Buttons **1**, **2**, **3** ❻. You select one of the buttons (turns blue) to set their Filter parameters, where you can enable it and configure it.

Now each Filter Button has a little LED ❼ on top that indicates if that Filter is enabled or not, so you don't have to actually click on it and see if the **ON** ❽ button is enabled.

Drag&Drop Hot Zones for Importing Audio

➡️ *Standard Method to Import Audio Files*

To import Audio Files into Alchemy requires the following steps:

- ☑ Switch to **ADVANCED** ❶ view
- ☑ Select a Source ❷ (**A, B, C, D**) where you want to import the audio file to
- ☑ *Click* on the Source Select Field ❸ and choose the **Import Audio** option
- ☑ In the next view that pops up, select an Analysis Mode ❺ at the lower-left corner.
- ☑ Select ❻ an audio file from the Browser or *drag* one from the Finder (or even directly from the **Loop Browser**) onto the Drop Zone.

➡️ *New Method*

Now you can drag an audio file from the Finder or from inside Logic directly onto the Sources area.

- ▸ **Global**: If Global ❼ (or **Morph**) is selected in the sidebar, *dragging* a file over the Sources area will change the individual Source to a field of four hot zones ❽. *Dragging* over a specific zone (**Additive, Spectral, Granular, Sampler**) highlights that zone and determines the Analysis Mode for the audio file import when you release the mouse button.

- ▸ **Source**: If one of the four Sources ❾ (**A, B, C, D**) is selected in the sidebar, then the area switches to the four hot zones ❿ when you drag an audio file over, providing the four Analysis Modes for importing that audio file into that Source.

More Alchemy Changes

Here is a list of more smaller changes in the Alchemy Plugin:

- ☑ It is now possible to set the value of the FM, Comb or Ring Mod filters to a MIDI note value to precisely tune it. The filters now also offer much higher resolution.
- ☑ Alchemy's additive synthesis engine has been updated, resulting in greater clarity and improved tuning stability when using Resynthesis.
- ☑ Scrolling in Alchemy now responds correctly when Natural Scrolling is enabled in the System settings.
- ☑ Alchemy now uses the same zoom commands as other areas of Logic Pro.
- ☑ The Modulation Rack now offers a menu from which any already modulated target may be chosen.
- ☑ Controls for unused modules are now dimmed.
- ☑ The Spectral Edit display now includes time markers.
- ☑ Tempo grid lines are now shown when adjusting time alignment markers if the Position knob is being modulated by a tempo-synced source.
- ☑ Dragged points in the MSEG graph now snap to smaller time positions as the view is zoomed in.
- ☑ Modulation Edit buttons are now only visible if there is a modulator to edit.
- ☑ Clicking the Edit button for poly mod arp sources now displays the appropriate Poly Mod row.
- ☑ The AHDSR envelope display now shows two envelopes - one with the static parameter settings and another with the modulated version.
- ☑ When the mod wheel is assigned to a Perform control, an orange arc will appear around the knob and the modulated value will reflect the position of the mod wheel.
- ☑ Alchemy's MSEG editor now defaults to showing four beats.
- ☑ The default positions for non-standard filter types, such a Comb Filter are now 0%.
- ☑ Points added to MSEG or MODMAP graphs can now be moved as soon as they are created.
- ☑ When the AHDSR is in sync mode, dragged envelope points now automatically snap to points that are supported by the currently selected grid pattern.
- ☑ When the AHDSR is in sync mode, dragged envelope points now automatically snap to points that are supported by the currently selected grid pattern.

Alchemy Fixes and Improvements

Here is the list with all the small bugs and inconstancies that have been fixed:

- ☑ Saving Alchemy presets no longer sometimes causes unchanged AAZ files to sometimes be saved.
- ☑ Alchemy tracks created in GarageBand for iOS that use pitch bend now sound the same when played back in Logic Pro.
- ☑ Enabling Additive Synthesis in addition to an imported waveform using Spectral + Formant no longer sometimes results in unexpectedly loud output.
- ☑ The FM Filter no longer sometimes introduces a small amount of distortion even when the modulation amount is set to zero.
- ☑ Alchemy's import file browser again sorts items correctly.
- ☑ It is no longer possible to step through presets in the Alchemy library on a frozen track, which could lead to the sound changing unexpectedly when the track was unfrozen.
- ☑ Stepping through samples or folders using the Source left/right buttons now selects the samples and folders in the correct order.
- ☑ Activating Morph Mode on VA sources no longer sometimes causes the sync parameter to be set incorrectly,
- ☑ Importing a second EXS file to the same group no longer also creates an empty group in addition to the imported group.
- ☑ It is again possible to place the Start loop marker at the same position as the End loop marker.
- ☑ The delay when turning on morphing which sometimes occurs when using multisample EXS files is greatly reduced.
- ☑ Changing the Decay Curve in the AHDSR no longer sometimes changes the Attack, Hold and overall length.
- ☑ In the Keymap and Additive editors, dragging the sample end marker past the edge of a warp marker now causes the display to resize properly, and warp markers remain properly aligned with the audio waveform.
- ☑ Browser in Alchemy now continue to have scroll inertia immediately after a new preset is selected.
- ☑ Files listed in the Import File browser are again sorted as expected.
- ☑ Releasing the mouse button after drawing on the Spectral Canvas no longer causes a small gap in the audio.
- ☑ Moving the Transform Pad puck in Advanced mode no longer causes meters in Logic Pro to temporarily freeze.
- ☑ The Pitch Correction window now displays correctly when switching from one Source to another.
- ☑ Modulating Morph X/Y with an MSEG no longer sometimes causes clicks at the beginning of notes.
- ☑ Scrolling in Alchemy now responds correctly when Natural Scrolling is enabled in the System settings.

Changes and Improvements for Various Plugins

Here is a list changes and improvements in various Plugins:

ChromaVerb

☑ Undo and Redo now work with Damping EQ Curves in ChromaVerb

SpaceDesigner

☑ The resolution for IR waveforms is increased in Space Designer.

Phat FX

☑ Inserting a plug-in before an instance of Phat FX or Step FX, or moving Phat FX or Step FX to a different plug-in slot no longer removes automation for the master section of the plug-ins.

Channel EQ

☑ The Channel EQ UI now remains responsive after switching from Logic Pro to another application and then back when the Channel EQ has focus.

☑ Oversampling is no longer disabled in the Channel EQ when Linear Phase is toggled.

MatchEQ

☑ In the Match EQ plug-in, the Apply value no longer jumps back to 100% after it has been adjusted, and then a different reference file is learned or loaded.

Pitch Shifter

☑ The Pitch Shifter plug-in now reliably retains Manual timing settings when a project is saved and then reopened.

Test Oscillator

☑ Frequency values above 20 kHz typed into the Test Oscillator plug-in are now reliably maintained when the project is saved and then re-opened.

Scripter

☑ When two instances of Scripter are inserted on the same channel strip, removing one instance no longer sometimes causes the other instance to revert to a saved state.

☑ Scripter now reliably passes parameter values from menu controls to slider controls showing the same parameter.

MIDI Transposer

☑ With a User scale selected, the MIDI Transposer now immediately outputs the correct notes after changing the root note.

➡️ Drum Machine Designer

- ☑ It is now easier to drag items from one page to another in Drum Machine Designer.
- ☑ Undo now works after dragging a sample onto a cell in Drum Machine Designer.
- ☑ When dragging a sample onto Drum Machine Designer a cell, it is no longer possible to accidentally drop the sample onto the background instead of a specific cell, causing an error.
- ☑ Loading a new sound into a cell in Drum Machine Designer no longer disables the Reverb knob in Smart Controls.

➡️ Vintage Organ

- ☑ The Harmonics button for the Touch Bar for the Vintage Organ now continues to work after the first time it has been used.
- ☑ A long press on a pedal set to control the Leslie in the Vintage Organ now brakes the Leslie.

➡️ Studio Strings

- ☑ The Touch Bar now displays more articulations with channel strips using Studio Strings.
- ☑ Selecting an articulation for Studio Strings from the Touch Bar no longer sometimes assigns the adjacent articulation.

➡️ Studio Horns

- ☑ Changes to Vibrato Mode in Studio Horns are now consistent whether in Playback or Live mode.

➡️ General

- ☑ Key commands now work as expected when a value pop-up is visible for a knob in the Pedalboard.
- ☑ Pitch bends with a long ramp time now sound smoother with software instruments and AudioUnits instruments.
- ☑ Using compare in a plug-in now loads the correct setting after Save As has been performed.
- ☑ AudioUnit plug-ins in GarageBand for iOS songs opened in Logic Pro now retain their settings, if the equivalent Audio Unit plug-in is installed on the computer.
- ☑ The Brass Ensemble sampler instrument now reliably produces sound after being downloaded.

7 - Miscellaneous

Import / Export

Import

- ☑ Logic Pro now reliably imports all audio tracks for Multicam clips in Final Cut Pro XML files.
- ☑ Multichannel audio files that do not contain surround sound layout information are now imported as multiple individual tracks.
- ☑ Undo after importing audio tracks now also undoes the track naming performed upon import.
- ☑ Undo now works correctly after importing a track from a project into a Folder in another project.
- ☑ There is now an option to Keep Bus Number when importing tracks from another project.

Export

- ☑ Polyphonic parts are again properly exported in Music XML files.
- ☑ Double-clicking in the Bounce In Place dialog no longer unexpectedly starts a bounce.
- ☑ The start time for bouncing an entire project is now set correctly when the project starts earlier than 1 1 1 1.
- ☑ Music XML files exported from Logic Pro now includes chord symbols.

MIDI Controller/ Control Surface

- ☑ The Learn button in the Controller Assignments window now properly displays its status when the window is in Easy view.
- ☑ It is again possible to clear Clip indicators on Mackie Control compatibles control surfaces by pressing CTRL + Name/Value on the device.
- ☑ Triggering a command from a control surface that is not available in the current view now triggers an explanation warning.
- ☑ It is again possible to assign controls for the Arpeggiator plug-in to controls on MIDI controllers and Control Surfaces.
- ☑ It is again possible to Learn a Controller Assignment without opening the Controller Assignment window by pressing Command and L and then sending signal from the desired control device.
- ☑ The channel strip signal level LEDs on Mackie Control MCU Pro control surfaces no longer remains illuminated when changing fader banks.
- ☑ The return time on control surface level meters is no longer unexpectedly slow.
- ☑ The scrub and shuttle wheel now work with Mackie HUI and Tascam US-2400 control surfaces.
- ☑ It is now possible to use a Control Surface to control plug-ins and sends on an Aux channel that is not assigned to a Track.
- ☑ Channels selected on an MCU compatible control surface after setting a channel to Write mode are no longer sometimes also unexpectedly set to Write mode.
- ☑ Controller assignments mapped to TouchOSC Bridge no longer lose the mapping if the TouchOSC port is temporarily not available.

There are only three changes in the Preferences and Project Settings with the Logic Pro X v10.4.2 update.

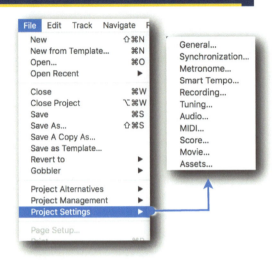

Project Settings

 **Smart Tempo**

The Smart Tempo page has a new Options sections with two settings for Smart Tempo Multitrack Sets and Export Tempo Resolution.

BTW. When the checkbox is enabled, then Logic will create an Edit Group not only when creating Smart Tempo Multitrack Sets.
I explain all the details in the Smart Tempo section of this manual.

Smart Tempo Project Settings

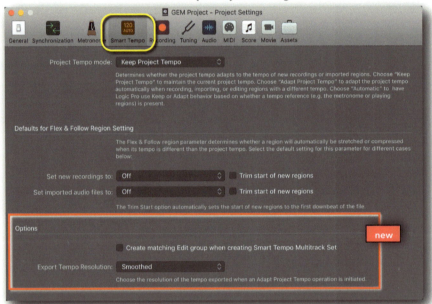

 **Score ➤ Layout**

The Score ➤ Layout page has a new section with four settings related to the Automatic Slurs
I explain that in the Automatic Slur section of this menu.

Score Project Settings

Preferences

 *Recording*

The menu item "**Create Track**" has been renamed to "**Create New Track**" for the Overlapping Recordings settings.

Recording Preferences

Main Menus

There are almost no changes in the various Main Menus.

➡ *Edit Menu*

The **Tempo** submenu has a couple of changes due to the update of the Smart Tempo feature.

➡ *Record Menu*

The menu item in the **Overlapping Audio Regions** submenu has been renamed from "**Create Track**" to "**Create New Track**".

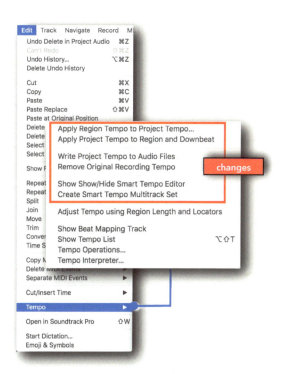

One of the 22 Key Command categories has been renamed.

File Tempo Editor is now **Smart Tempo Editor** ❺

New - Renamed - Moved

New Key Commands

Here are the new Key Commands listed in their individual category:

Attention: Use the **Initialize Unused** command from the Key Command's Action Menu to update all the new Key Commands without affecting any Key Commands that you have customized ("used").

🟡 **Global Commands**
- ▶ Delete Selected Groups
- ▶ Delete Unused Groups
- ▶ Select Members of Selected Groups
- ▶ Add Selected Channel Strips to Selected Groups
- ▶ Remove Selected Channel Strips from Selected Groups
- ▶ Copy Group Settings
- ▶ Paste Group Settings

🟡 **Main Window Tracks and Various Editors**
- ▶ Open Articulation Editor
- ▶ Set Marquee to Selection
- ▶ Select And Operate using Transform User Preset 1...32

🟡 **Main Window Tracks**
- ▶ Store Track Header Configuration as User Default
- ▶ Apply Track Header Configuration User Default
- ▶ Revert to Track Header Configuration Factory Default

🟡 **Mixer**
- ▶ Sends on Faders - On/Off
- ▶ Sends on Faders - Next Send
- ▶ Sends on Faders - Previous Send
- ▶ Sends on Faders - Cycle Through Sends
- ▶ Sends on Faders - Cycle Through Returns

🟡 **Score Editor**
- ▶ Convert Auto Slur
- ▶ Reset Auto Slur
- ▶ Slur Auto Direction
- ▶ Auto Slur Above
- ▶ Auto Slur Below
- ▶ Slur Last Note
- ▶ Slur(s) for non-contiguous selected notes

🟡 **Smart Tempo Editor**
- ▶ Set Downbeat to Playhead Position

Renamed/Removed Key Commands

Here is the list of Key Commands that have been renamed or removed:

● *Main Window Tracks and Various Editors*

Many of the Smart Tempo commands have been renamed or removed. This also causes some changes in that category. The following four commands have been removed.

▶ **Adapt Project Tempo to Region Tempo and Align to Downbeat**
▶ **Adapt Project Tempo to Region Tempo and Align to Beat**
▶ **Adapt Project Tempo and All Regions to Region Tempo and Downbeat**
▶ **Adapt Project Tempo to Region Tempo**

... and these are the two commands they are replacing them:

▶ **Apply Region Tempo to Project Tempo...**
▶ **Apply Project Tempo to Region and Downbeat**

● *Smart Tempo Editor*

The following three commands have been removed from the Smart Tempo Editor category because they were either redundant or confusing with other Key Commands:

▶ **Start or Stop Playback** *opt+spacebar* was removed. You can use the existing Key Command **Preview** which has the same Key Equivalent *opt+spacebar*.
▶ **Toggle Cylce** (yes, this is how it was was misspelled) is also obsolete. The existing Key Command **Cycle Audition On/Off** with the same Key Equivalent **^C** can be used instead. That command also works in the Audio File Editor and the Project Audio Browser.
▶ **Toggle Catch** was another redundant Key Command to toggle the Catch Playhead Button ▸▾◂ in the Smart Tempo Editor. It was removed because the existing Key Command **Catch Playhead Position** can be used when the Smart Tempo Editor has key focus.
▶ **Select from Start to Cursor** renamed to **Select from Start to Playhead**
▶ **Select from Cursor to End** renamed to **Select from Playhead to End**
▶ **Center around Cursor** renamed to **Center around Playhead**

● *Main Window Tracks and Various Editors ➤ Various Editor*

The Key Command **Catch Playhead Position** was moved from the **Main Window Tracks and Various Editors** category to the **Various Editors** category.

Key Commands Sets

The Actions Button ❶ in the upper-left corner of the Key Commands Window opens a menu with various commands to manage the Key Commands. The functionality for the two menu items **Import Key Commands...** and **Import Key Commands to Selection...** ❷ has changed.

Now, when you import a Key Commands Set ❸, it will also automatically copied ❹ to the folder where all the custom Key Commands Sets are stored *~/Music/Audio Music Apps/Key Commands/*.

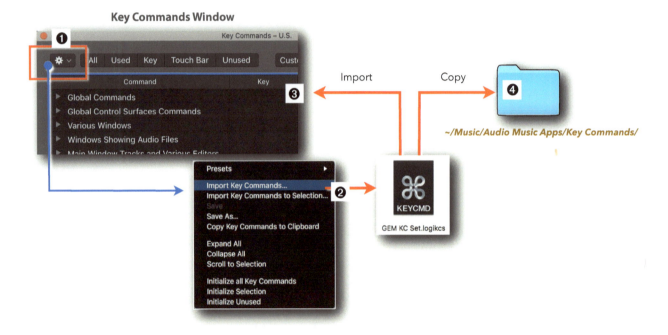

Asterisk * for Key Command-only commands

The dot ❺ in front of a Key Command that indicates that this command only exists as a Key Command and not as a Menu Command is now replaced with an asterisk (*) ❻ after the Key Command.

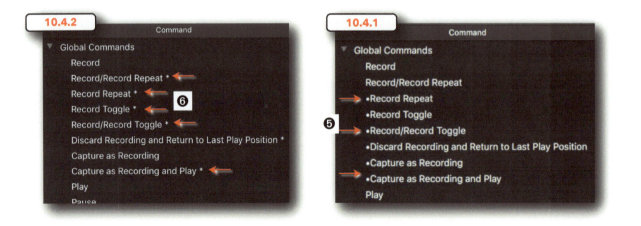

Conclusion

This concludes my manual *"Logic Pro X - What's New in 10.4.2"*.

If you find my visual approach to explaining features and concepts helpful, please recommend my books to others or maybe write a review on Amazon or the iBooks Store. This will help me to continue this series.
To check out other books in my "Graphically Enhanced Manuals" series, go to my website at:
www.DingDingMusic.com/Manuals

To contact me directly, email me at GEM@DingDingMusic.com

More information about my day job as a composer and links to my social network sites are on my website:
www.DingDingMusic.com

  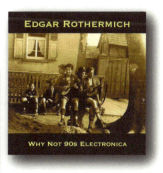

Listen to my music on SoundCloud

Thanks for your interest and your support,

Edgar Rothermich